THE GLENS OF ANTRIM

Their Folklore and History

Michael Sheane

ARTHUR H. STOCKWELL LTD
Torrs Park   Ilfracombe   Devon
Established 1898

D1549884

British Library Cataloguing-in-Publication Data.
A catalogue record for this book is available
from the British Library.

By the same author:
Ulster & Its Future After the Troubles (1977)
Ulster & The German Solution (1978)
Ulster & The British Connection (1979)
Ulster & The Lords of the North (1980)
Ulster & The Middle Ages (1982)
Ulster & St Patrick (1984)
The Twilight Pagans (1990)
Enemy of England (1991)
The Great Siege (2002)
Ulster in the Age of Saint Comgall of Bangor (2004)
Ulster Blood (2005)
King William's Victory (2006)
Ulster Stock (2007)
Famine in the Land of Ulster (2008)
Pre-Christian Ulster (2009)

914.
16

ISBN 978-0-7223-3996-1
Printed in Great Britain by
Arthur H. Stockwell Ltd
Torrs Park   Ilfracombe
Devon

Contents

Introduction

The Glens of Antrim stretch from Glenarm village in the south to Ballycastle in the north. Throughout there is a spectacular view of Scotland. Inland, the Glens rise up to form the Antrim Plateau. Today the coast road stretches along the way, but at the beginning of the nineteenth century there was no road; journeys had to be taken inland to Larne or by curragh (a skin-covered boat).

As a teenager I travelled extensively in the Glens, and when I was old enough to drive a motorbike I would make the journey to Cushendall and back to Ballygally along the coast road.

The coast road stretches for about twenty-five miles and its construction was a great engineering feat. In places the road was blasted through the rocks – for example, the Black Arch, outside Larne, and the Red Arch, near Garron Point.

Today the Glens are not isolated: the journey to Larne, where there is a market every Wednesday, takes about forty-five minutes by car.

Since earliest times there have been close trading connections between the Glens and Scotland. Both Glenarm and Carnlough have little harbours where ships still dock. It was perhaps easier to travel to Scotland from the Glens at the beginning of the nineteenth century than to travel to Larne and other parts of County Antrim.

The comings and goings between the Glens and Scotland (particularly Argyllshire) mean that today many of the Glens folk of County Antrim look across the North Channel to the Mull of

Kintyre to trace their roots. The MacDonnell family, of Scots origin, were from the fifteenth century onwards Lords of the Glens as well as Lords of the Scots Isles.

The journey from the Antrim coast to the Mull of Kintyre and Campbeltown, in the days of sail, took several hours. Since an early date there has always been a ferry between Stranraer and Larne. The Scottish connection was regarded with suspicion by the English authorities, for the Glens folk tried to establish a separate political entity in the east of County Antrim. Elizabeth I, in the sixteenth century, was particularly troubled by the Scots of the Glens of Antrim.

The coast road was built in the 1830s not only to ease communications with Larne; it was also built as a military road, to keep an eye on the Scots of the Glens. However, the Glens still remained a place apart, and today travelling from Larne and Ballygally it is easy to see the cultural differences between the middle-class towns of Ballygally and Larne and the Catholic communities of the Glens.

Gaelic was spoken in the Glens up to the beginning of the twentieth century, and many of the old customs and traditions continue. The Glens folk, it was claimed in the 1831 Ordnance Survey, were people apart – quite unlike those from the Protestant parishes of the south of the county. Their features, manner and accent were different.

The Glens folk were noted for their honesty. Theft was hardly known, and all kinds of property lay about unprotected. The men of the Glens could trace their history back to the age of Shane O'Neill, a Gaelic lord who was killed by the MacDonnells of Antrim, and whose head was sent to adorn the gates of Dublin Castle. It is thought that he was buried at Glenarm.

At the beginning of the nineteenth century the Glens of Antrim were a nest of smugglers and pirates who operated without fear of the authorities.

Before the coast road was built, Larne, Glenarm and Carnlough were joined by a road that went up and down the various headlands. The road was extremely muddy and treacherous, with steep slopes, and this made transport by cart very difficult in the best of weather. The road along to Pathfoot towards Glenarm was extremely dangerous after dark: in places it was unfenced, and horse riders sometimes fell over the cliffs to their death. The path was not recommended either in summer or in winter. In many places it was essential to have guides. For some years travellers had reported to London and Dublin that the Glens folk could only with difficulty take a cart to market in the summer, and in winter they might be isolated for weeks through the effect of rain on the steep mountain tracks.

The lack of good communication between the Glens and the rest of the county helped to strengthen the already close links with Scotland. The people of Cushendun imported many of their goods from Scotland, rather than transporting them over the treacherous roads from Carrickfergus.

An eighteenth-century traveller from Larne to Glenarm would have passed through the village of Carncastle to the steep hill known as the Path. Horses were available at a house (now owned by Hugh O'Neill) at the bottom of the Path, to help travellers up the steep slope. Before these horses were used, local hands were expected to push the gentry's carriages up the hill. Once the top of the Path had been reached, the traveller passed by Dickey's Town and down the steep hill leading to Glenarm village.

In 1841, when Mr and Mrs S. C. Hall visited Glenarm they talked with an old man whose coach and six horses had been caught on the muddy hill. They unharnessed the six horses, and the beasts got on well enough when they had nothing heavier than themselves to carry; the rich people got out and walked; and some men arrived from the Glens to draw the carriage up the hill. "Oh, my God, we managed it rightly," the old man told them.

In 1832 Lieutenant Thomas Hore wrote that the coast road was quite hilly with the exception of that part near Glenarm – the Path – a road of terrifying steepness.

The Glens were opened up with the construction of the Grand Military Road along the coast. William Bald, a Scotsman, was the principal engineer of this great achievement.

The section from Larne to Cushendall runs mostly along the foot of the cliffs. Here Bald devised a method of blasting the chalk cliffs so that the huge rocks rested at the water's edge, making a foundation. In his 1835 Ordnance Survey, James Boyle mentions that a part of the lime road from Glenarm, under the supervision of the Board of Works, had just been opened, so now the dreadful hill of the Path could be avoided. The construction of the new road to Larne benefited the farmers of the parish, for they could now more easily take their produce to the market. The Path had hitherto been a hindrance to trade.

The total cost of constructing the coast road was £37,000. In 1978 a plaque was erected on the coast road at the Halfway House between Glenarm and Larne in commemoration of Bald's achievement. It states that the coast road was constructed between 1832 and 1842 by the men of the Glens under the direction of William Bald. When the road was constructed Halfway House was built so that passengers could stop for refreshment.

A mail cart would transport about a dozen passengers back to back so they could drink in the scenery of the Antrim coast. The Halfway House is now a pub and a hotel.

Since the construction of the coast road, the road has been closed many times between Larne and Carnlough because of landslides as the area has been eroded by the sea. In February 1967 over 200 tons of rubble slipped into the causeway at Glenarm, but a new causeway was built about ninety feet away from the cliffs towards the sea. For this, 255,000 tons of basalt and limestone were transported from a quarry at White Bay to make a foundation in the sea. The new road was opened in June 1968, but four months later it too was swept away in a storm. A local poet at this time said that the erection of a new road was a mistake, but since that date the Antrim coast road has remained in use.

The people of the Glens are noted for their generosity. They are obliging, peaceable and well conducted, but they are sometimes over-fond of alcohol. When the coast road was built, the English language was barely understood in the Glens, and most of the people spoke Irish. Those that did speak English spoke it very well, free from any accent.

The historian H. V. Morton in his book *In search of Ireland* has told of the beauty of this stretch – there was no other road like it in the British Isles. A poem of H. Browne has praised the men who built this road from Larne to Cushendall and its spectacular scenery. The poem describes the glories of Glenariff, the crags of Garron Point, the shingled beaches, the sandy shores, the whins in glory, the distant misty headlands, the Glens and the winding way, the great view of the Mull of Kintyre in Scotland, the screaming gulls and the lash of the angry spray. 'The man that planned the roadway had kept all these matters in view, but . . . a fairy sat on his shoulder and told him what to do.'

At Glenarm, where the MacDonnells had their fine castle, the storied past was peopled with fairies, and even today the coast road has a suggestion of fairyland about it.

The coast has many headlands of basalt and limestone, and in places the road has been tunnelled through the rock. The Black Arch, about two miles outside Larne, was built to allow only single-decker vehicles through, but still it is an impressive sight. One has only to visit the little communities of Ballygally, Glenarm and Carnlough to obtain a glimpse of the beautiful scenery.

During the nineteenth century on spring days you could not miss the strong smell of burning kelp along this stretch of coast. Kelp-burning was one of Ulster's oldest industries, and there was a flourishing trade along the Antrim coast. The demand for kelp came from two separate sources: in agriculture it was used for generations as a fertiliser (fresh seaweed is as rich in nitrogen and other nutrients as cow manure), and in photography it was used in making light-sensitive paper, owing to its high iodine content. The greatest demand for kelp came from the photographic industry in Scotland. The kelp was known as *berros*. It was collected during the winter months and left to dry on the rocks. After a while it was turned over and then placed in bundles to enable air to circulate below. The bundles were then put on top of iron bars which lay across the stone kilns. These kilns were different from lime kilns. They consisted of four crude walls about three feet high, three feet wide and fifteen feet long. A fire was kindled under the bar grating, and the intense heat broke down the seaweed.

The industry was in decline by the turn of the twentieth century. In 1935 the *Larne Times* reported that hundreds of tons of seaweed were rotting on the beaches between Ballygally Head and Garron Point. In previous years men and boys had gathered, dried and burned the kelp, but now they stated that the price paid would not compensate them for their trouble. What was formerly a lucrative trade was now passing away along the Antrim coast. Kelp was no longer widely used either for top-dressing pasture land or for ploughing into the soil before planting.

As a grammar-school boy at Larne I often marvelled at the Black

Arch. A little path, for those on foot, circles round the east side of the arch. The Black Arch seems to be in better condition than the Red Arch, which is about twenty miles up the coast at Red Bay. The 162 service bus just fitted under the two arches.

Beyond the Black Arch lies the little village of Drains Bay. The original Irish name for Drains Bay was Cuan an Dhroighneain ('the bay of the blackthorns').

At the top of the Glenarm road there is a view of the North Channel, and Scotland. From here you can see the Maidens lighthouses – two lighthouses built on rocks close to each other. Only one is in service. From the Larne–Cairnryan ferry on a dark night the flashing light can be clearly seen.

As a teenager, in my father's speedboat, we would make trips from Ballygally out to the Maidens, but there were many treacherous rocks that had to be looked out for.

Carnfunnock, a country park, was opened at the end of the 1980s. Today there is a café with a tremendous view of the North Channel. Here there is the Ulster Way, a walk through the forests, and an information centre and shop, where some books on Ulster's past and present can be bought. There is a car park, and cars and buses climb up the slight incline from the coast road to the café. There are also camping facilities.

Ballygally Head lies only a few miles from Carnfunnock. It rises 300 feet above sea level. In the fifties it was open grassland, but now there is a golf course and clubhouse. There are high rocks or stacks off the coast near the hairpin bend of Ballygally Head, and here climbers can be seen, despite warnings from Larne Borough Council. Just before the stacks is a quarry rising about 100 feet above the road. Between the shore and the quarry is a stone wall; perhaps the stones were quarried nearby.

The wind is strong as one turns the hairpin, and the first sight that comes in view is O'Halloran's Castle. Here a poet called Agnew is supposed to have lived. The castle is situated on a rock about 100 yards from the road, but the walls have been plundered for stone to build other dwellings. A novel called *O'Halloran, or, The Insurgent Chief* has been written about the castle. The novel was written in 1820 and the author, a Larne doctor called James McHenry, would not have known that after his death people would take his tale as fact. It deals with the rising of the United Irishmen in 1798 along the coast from Larne to Ballygally. The old stone building at the top of the hairpin at Ballygally Head features in this book as the rendezvous for the rebels, and O'Halloran is described as an honourable County Antrim gentleman. Over the years the building became known as O'Halloran's Castle, although no such person existed. His character is thought to have been modelled on James Agnew Farrell, the leader of the rebels, who also bought quarries at Magheramorne. The tale is centred around the rising in 1798, but the story is mainly a romantic novel. O'Halloran's sister Ellen and Edward Barrymore, an English gentleman, provide the main romantic story. Few copies of the book remain today.

James McHenry, the author of *O'Halloran*, was born in Dunluce Street, Larne, in what was then known as Livingstone's Court. His parents were George McHenry and Mary Smiley. As a child he suffered a severe back injury which left him a hunchback. He was quite sensitive about this deformity, and it was one of the reasons he became a surgeon rather than following his parents' wishes and becoming a minister of religion. He practised for several years as a doctor in Belfast.

On one of his tours around Carncastle he met and married a sixteen-year-old girl, Jane Robinson of Glenarm. The wedding, which took place in 1816, was long-remembered in the region, for the doctor was twice the age of the young girl. *O'Halloran* was his most successful novel. He followed it up with *The Hearts of Steel*, which was a novel based on his own experiences. In 1798, when Dr McHenry was a boy, Larne was taken by the rebels, and he saw the fighting in the streets between the rebels and the troops. In 1825 he emigrated to the United States with his wife and two sons, and they settled in Philadelphia, where he became editor of the *American Monthly Magazine*. McHenry wrote many other works, including *The Usurper* and *The Bard of Erin*. In 1842 he was appointed American consul at Londonderry by President Tyler. His wife and family stayed in Philadelphia while he returned home to Ireland. As he rode around Larne on a wet day, Dr McHenry contracted an illness. His condition rapidly worsened, and all the doctors in the Larne area were called upon to offer their services where he lay stricken down at Stewart's Hotel – but all in vain. On 21 July the learned doctor died in Larne aged fifty-nine. He was buried by the side of his mother in the grounds of the church at Inver.

Beside O'Halloran's Castle there is a small rock where an old lady is said to have lived making soap out of seaweed. This rock and view of the castle make a good photograph. The old lady probably lived there before the castle was built.

As lads, Kenny Allen and I would make our way over the rocks around the castle, imagining times in old Ballygally. We would make the journey from O'Halloran's Castle around the hairpin of Ballygally Head to Carnfunnock, where we would meet up with Hugh Steel. Hugh lived with his father and mother in the lodge house of Lady Dixon's estate, Lady Dixon having vacated the house during the early fifties. Here there was a little forest, which I imagined to be a plantation, and we cut at the trees with little axes.

The middle-class settlement at Ballygally is a phenomenon of the thirties and forties. Earlier photographs of the village show only a few buildings, such as Day Dixon's Coachman's House and the much older Ballygally Castle.

Ballygally Castle.

Ballygally Castle dates back to the early seventeenth century. It is not really a castle, but a planter's bawn, with walls surrounding it to ward off attacks from the native population.

After visiting Ballygally in 1683, Richard Dobbs wrote that standing near the shore was James Shaw's castle (now known as Ballygally Castle). Shaw was a Scot and a planter or colonizer, and he had come from Scotland. The castle had been robbed by Tories or Irish outlaws from Londonderry.

A road runs from the castle to Carncastle, where there are three churches – St Patrick's (Anglican), the Unitarian church and the Presbyterian church. They lie about a mile up the Carncastle road; St Patrick's is remote from the other two churches.

The castle at Ballygally was built in 1625 by Captain James (John) Shaw, and it is typical of the small Scottish style of house built in many townlands in Ulster. On a stone over one of the doors is inscribed the date when the castle was built, Captain Shaw's wife's name and the Shaw coat of arms. The castle has three stories, connected by a winding stone staircase inside the back of the building. James Shaw (or John as he is sometimes referred to in some documents) came from Greenock in Scotland in 1606 to take advantage of the planting that was being carried out in Ulster at the beginning of the seventeenth century. He applied for a grant from the Earl of Antrim, and a grant was made on 21 February 1621 to James Shaw the younger of Carnfunnock and 'the north part of Corkermain, and the south part of Ballyrudder'. A grant was also made to John Shaw the elder, of Ballygally, of 'eighteen score' acres of land, and another grant of 'small lands' was made on 1 February 1643.

In 1641 John Shaw fortified Ballygally Castle, for the Gaels rose up in rebellion against the policies of the British Government, which had taken land away from the Irish and handed it to the planters or colonizers.

In 1680 the castle was again attacked. The castle was quite small, and morale was probably not high within its walls as the defenders fired at the rebels. The Gaels hated the planters and their Scots background, and they came down the steep road from the Antrim Hills armed with sticks and primitive swords. The sons and descendants of the native Irish who had been dispossessed by the settlement scheme, and who had been cut down following the rising of 1641, were determined to take revenge against the English and Scots who had usurped their lands. These rebels were called Tories. It was recorded that Ballygally Castle was attacked by the Tories of Londonderry, and that it was robbed and plundered. The castle may have been under siege for some time. The Tories perhaps slipped back into the woods after sacking the building. A £5 reward was offered to anyone who killed a Tory.

In 1786 John Shaw, a great-great grandson of the first Captain Shaw held the castle; he was married but without heirs. His sister was married to Dr McCullough, who lived in Larne, about five miles to the south of Ballygally. At this date Larne was developing into a substantial port to Scotland, and curraghs plied along the Antrim coast to avoid the Tory outlaws who frequented the land. It was alleged that Dr McCullough forced John Shaw to sign a forged will leaving his possessions, including the castle, to him. Then the doctor killed him.

McCullough lived in Ballygally Castle for four years, and it is from this period that the ghost of the castle originates. The ghost is said to be that of his brother-in-law.

In 1790, John Shaw's nephew, Henry Shaw, through legal action, took possession of the castle, but following the uprising of 1798 he was arrested and confined in the Market House at Carrickfergus. He died in 1799 of natural causes and was succeeded by his son, William – the last of the Shaws to occupy the castle. William failed in a business enterprise in Belfast, and this prompted him to sell the castle in 1820 to Edward Jones Agnew of Kilwaughter Castle for the sum of £1,500.

While in the possession of the Agnew family the castle was occupied for several years as a coastguard station. The Reverend Classon Porter, a Presbyterian minister and historian, took up residence.

Major William Agnew lived in the castle for some time, and in 1938 the castle was extended and opened as a hotel.

During the mid-1950s it was owned by Cyril Lord, the textile magnate.

In 1969 it became known as the Candlelight Inn and was taken over by Hastings Ltd, Belfast.

Ballygally could be called the Gateway to the Glens, for Glenarm, the first glen, lies about ten miles up the coast road. There is a regular bus service from Larne to Cushendall, and the journey through the little coastal townlands is interesting. Ballygally has a population of about 600, and along with the settlement of the seafront there are more modern houses lying up the Croft Road. Prices of these houses are in the region of £200,000, and those on the seafront are roughly the same. Dominating the slight hill on the seafront is Harbinson's House, which is no longer in the possession of the Harbinson family.

As a child I would run up the long drive to the house to play with Chris Harbinson, for we were about the same age. We would climb Ballygally Head and make eight-minute home movies of Ballygally and the coast, as well as going camping at Cushendun, walking over the Antrim Hills to Newtown Crommelin and down Glendun to the Antrim coast. On one occasion we set off to cycle to Londonderry, but there was a lot of rain and we had to abandon the trip.

In the fifties my father built a GP 14 yacht and a speedboat, and bought a glass-fibre dinghy. A port was made on the rocky beach in front of our bungalow. At this time there were several little ports hacked out of the stone on the beach – Hunter's Port, Lough's Port and Law's Port. Although I was brought up by his sea, I could not swim, and my father was not too keen on my going out alone in the boats. I had to wear a life jacket, and I was alarmed when the wind filled the sail and the boat heeled over. We would sail along the coast, mostly in the speedboat, to the little harbour at Glenarm, where ships still load up with limestone bound for Scotland.

Ballygally means 'the townland of the rocks', but old photographs show Ballygally with a strand but no houses yet built. A horse and cart would load up with seaweed, or wrack, and this was extensively used for fertilizing the land.

Ballygally Head is of volcanic origin. The headland rises about 300 feet above the bay.

From the window of our bungalow I often looked across to the Mull of Kintyre in the distance, and I often wondered what Scotland was like. I dreamed of taking the Stranraer ferry from Larne, to enjoy the three-hour journey to the Scottish port. From Stranraer trains run to Dumfries, Glasgow and Carlisle (in England).

Also connected with Ballygally is the tale of Jean Park. The story goes that a boat once drifted into Ballygally Bay, and in it were a woman and a little baby. The woman was dead but the baby, not a day old, was alive. Where they had come from no one knew. A coastguard took the baby home and called her Marina Jane. She grew up to be a beautiful woman and she married a sailor called Park. For many years after the marriage, her husband was both a sailor and a farmer, and they were content.

When he was absent on one of his voyages, Jane had a dream that her husband would never return, but daily she would go down to the beach to look for signs of the boat bringing him back to her. This went on for a long time. The farm was neglected and her husband never returned. Kindly neighbours did what they could for her, but the inevitable happened – bailiffs arrived. Jane was evicted from her home, and it was boarded up. With her own hands she built a hut and gathered limpets for food. She had a faithful dog called Brinie that seldom left her side. The dog had four puppies in their hut on Ballygally Beach.

Ballygally Head and Strand.

One night a great storm blew up and she awoke. A neighbour tried to persuade Jane to come to their house for shelter, but she preferred not to leave in case her husband turned up. Her dog tried to pull her by her dress, but Jane would not leave. Next morning there was no sign of Jane or her hut. She had come from the sea, and to the sea she had returned.

Rising above Ballygally village is the impressive mountain of Knockdhu, which along with Ballygally Head has yielded evidence of a Stone Age man. The Carncastle road from Ballygally runs past the churches and then up past Knockdhu. There is a quarry here where Stone Age man fashioned his weaponry and tools.

Very often I travelled this road on foot or on my motorbike. The road leads on over the Antrim Hills to Aughafatten, Carnalbanagh, and Newtown Crommelin, and down into Glendun, where it reaches the Antrim coast. I went camping in this area in a little green tent with my friend Chris Harbinson, and generally the rain stayed away (except for that trip to Londonderry).

The headlands of Glenarm Head, Garron Point and Torr Head can be seen from Ballygally Bay before one travels the inland route. There is a dramatic view of Ballygally from the top of the road leading into the Antrim Hills. It is an enviable place to live. One can imagine ancient man taking the inland route and watching ships and curraghs coming from the Mull of Kintyre. On a dark night, the Maidens lighthouse lights up the horizon and makes travelling the Knockdhu road dramatic.

In the forest at Deer Park there is a river, and water is available for the thirsty, but there are often lots of flies.

The Iron Age settlement at Knockdhu dates back to about 500 BC, and some of the finds indicate a society where the chieftains were quite wealthy – for example, decorative horse trappings and scabbards. Following a study of Knockdhu, at the Sallagh Braes (also overlooking Ballygally Bay), Richard Hodges of Southampton University found what must be one of the most important Iron Age sites in Ireland. The area around the mountain shows evidence of much activity.

Nearby at Linford are two ring-ditched burrows – low burial mounds, each surrounded by a circular trench with an outer embankment in which the ashes of the dead were buried in clay urns. To the west of these burrows are a series of pits with their sides cast in iron, suggesting that they were probably mines.

According to Hodges, Knockdhu was once the centre of a market or fair for foreign goods as well as serving local traders who might have been attracted here by the Iron Age industry. Local iron goods would have been exchanged by interested traders for specialized manufactured articles such as horse gear.

There is an impressive hill fort at Deer Park, lying in a field belonging to Jim Davidson. Archeologists from the Historic Buildings Branch (DOE), started to excavate the site in 1985. The raised rath or ring fort was fifteen feet high and 144 feet in diameter at its base. The rath dates back to AD 500 (the early Christian period). It was, in fact, a series of defended homesteads built one on top of another, so as the archaeologists dug downwards they were going back in time from AD 1000 to AD 500. This dig is perhaps the most important dig to have taken place in Ireland, and it has provided many insights into early life here. Although the mound was a defended homestead, not everyone lived on sites such as this; it is quite possible that they were for only the richer members of the community – those who had property worth defending.

The excavations at Deer Park have led to a number of interesting discoveries: clear outlines of round-based houses with kerbed fireplaces; two souterrains (underground chambers) lined with stones and covered with lintels; much coarse locally made pottery; evidence of metalworking, such as slag from iron-smelting and pieces of silver; and a glass button. There were also flint tools, polished stone axes and tools for sharpening knives. Other finds indicate that they made their own clothes and ground their own flour.

One of the most spectacular finds has been the remains of a wattle-walled house – the only preserved wattle house in Ireland. The walls are made of hazel twigs, woven carefully to provide maximum strength. The coordinator of the dig, Chris Lynn, explained that between the outside wall and the inside the occupants crammed all manner of materials to serve as insulation. Just like birds in their nests, they wanted warmth. The house would have had a central stone hearth where the families cooked their meals on a spit.

Island Magee is considered to have been the birthplace of Presbyterianism in Ireland. The foundations were laid here in 1613 when the Reverend Edward Brice came over from Scotland. Carncastle was one of the fourteen districts to which, following the meeting of the first presbytery at Carrickfergus, ministers that had arrived since the previous April with General Munro's Scottish army were sent.

Patrick Adair, a relative of the Adairs of Ballymena, was ordained as the first Presbyterian minister of Carncastle in May 1646 by the newly formed presbytery at Carrickfergus under the patronage of James Shaw of Ballygally Castle. Patrick Adair preached in the little church at Carncastle for fifteen years.

When the Presbyterian ministers of Antrim and Down broke with the Cromwellian parliament of 1649 and prayed for Charles II, who had promised to establish Presbyterianism in Ulster, they were removed from the parish churches. However, an Act of Uniformity in 1661, after the monarchy had been restored, drove Irish Presbyterians out of their church livings and led to the prohibition of kirk meetings and the exile of their ministers.

The Reverend Patrick Adair was ousted by the Bishop of Down and Connor, Jeremy Taylor, but he stayed behind and hid amongst the rocks at Carncastle, administering to his congregation for another fourteen years. In 1674 he was removed from Carncastle to a new ministry at Belfast.

After William III landed at Carrickfergus, on 14 June 1690, Adair headed a deputation from the Presbyterians of Ireland to address the King at Belfast Castle. Adair died in Belfast four years later.

John Campbell succeeded Patrick Adair in 1675, and was himself succeeded in 1714 by William Taylor.

Taylor was one of the four founding members of the Antrim Presbytery. The separation of the Antrim Presbytery from the General Synod took place in 1726, when William Taylor of Carncastle and his congregation separated from the larger and joined the smaller body.

John Lawson, who followed William Taylor, was ordained at Carncastle in 1728, and he administered to the congregation for fifteen years.

Since the 1940s both the Glenarm and Carncastle non-subscribing congregations have been amalgamated, and the congregation is proud that it worships in the oldest church in the area. The building is said to have been erected in 1688, although in 1779 it was rebuilt and enlarged. However, the present building is decaying and will have to be demolished soon, to be replaced by a modern church.

In 1829 no fewer than seventeen congregations seceded from the Synod of Ulster and formed themselves into a separate association called the Remonstrant Synod. Amongst these congregations was Carncastle. Other ministers and congregations continued to adhere to the Synod of Ulster. The subscribing, or orthodox, church, being now smaller in number, was ousted from its place of worship, but in 1831 they built their own church in Carncastle, and in the following year the Reverend James Carmichael was ordained as the first minister of the new church. On 25 May the first wedding took place in the church, when Owen married Jane Brow of Carncastle. Henry Shaw Ballyhacket was a witness.

A daughter of the Reverend Carmichael, Annie, married George McFerran, JP, of Drumnagreagh House, a prominent building on the road from Ballygally to Glenarm. George McFerran built the church walls and gates, as well as erecting a new school in 1901 and converting the old school into a teacher's residence. Two stained-glass windows were installed in the church in 1939 in memory of Mr and Mrs McFerran.

S. Edgar Stewart succeeded the Reverend Carmichael in 1871, and he was followed by a number of distinguished clerics.

St Patrick's Anglican Church was built at Carncastle in 1815. It is beautifully situated on a slight hill, but it is a very small building with stained-glass windows. The longest incumbent appears to have been the Reverend Denzil Caldwell. He retired from the parish in the late eighties. The Church of Ireland rectory lies about a mile away at the start of the Carncastle road at Ballygally.

As a child I attended religious instruction, but the numbers were not very great. Here I learned the fundamentals of the faith of the Church of Ireland (the Irish counterpart of its sister Church, the Church of England). The Roman Catholic church also lay at the beginning of the Carncastle road, but I was educated to believe in the Protestant faith.

St Patrick's stands near the site of a much older church, some remains of which can still be seen in the churchyard. The first mention of anyone ministering in this building was the Reverend Patrick Adair, the Presbyterian minister who was ejected in 1661. The Reverend Matthews, a Welshman, was installed in 1666.

In the latter half of the seventeenth century the parishes of Carncastle and Kilwaughter were united. For a number of years the rectors of these parishes were generally non-resident, and the clerical duties were carried out by resident curates. One of these curates was the Reverend Ralph Ward, who died in 1849. He was succeeded by his nephew, the Reverend Charles Ward, who became the first rector of the united parish with a curate, the Reverend J. Richardson, resident in Carncastle. It was soon after this that the ecclesiastical connection between these two parishes was discontinued. There is mention of a Reverend Woods after this, and it is known for certain that in 1881 the Reverend A. Phoenix started his twenty-year ministry at Carncastle. The baptismal font in the present church was once used by Dean Swift in the old church at Ballynure. Between 1694 and 1697, Swift, the author of *Gulliver's Travels,* lived by the shore at Carrickfergus and was in charge of the churches at Kilroot and Ballynure. Amongst those buried in the graveyard is the Reverend Classon Porter, the noted church historian.

There is a curious story connected with the Spanish chestnut tree in the graveyard of St Patrick's Church, Carncastle. The twisted branches of the tree are in contrast with the native trees and shrubs around it. It is said that it was planted from one of the ships of the Spanish Armada that came to grief further up the coast in 1588, after Spain tried to invade England. A body from one of galleons is said to have been washed ashore at Ballygally. In the pocket of the corpse were some chestnuts, which were buried with the body in the graveyard. The seed eventually germinated and grew into the great tree that can be seen today.

James Campbell, the weaver poet, was born in Carncastle in 1798 in a small hovel. His education was scant but he learned to read and write. While still a boy he learned the craft of weaving – a cottage industry common in the eighteenth century. He moved to Ballynure while still a young man to work at his trade, and he married a young Carrickfergus woman called Stewart. He set up home in Ballynure working at his hand loom. The pay was not very good, for he laboured eighty or ninety hours per week for ten or eleven shillings. While working at his loom he kept pen and paper handy so that he could write down the poetry as inspiration came. His songs and poems were widely read by the poor tenant farmers around Carncastle and Ballynure. He was a welcome visitor in any farmer's house. His poems dealt with everyday matters – a reason for their popularity. In those days it was common to find flitches and hams of home-cured bacon hanging from the kitchen rafters; also many houses would have a large barrel well filled with crushed meal from a neighbouring mill and a stack of peat for burning during the winter ready outside in the yard. It was everyday things such as these that Campbell wrote about in his verses.

When he was almost forty years of age Campbell joined the United Irishmen, who wanted civil and religious liberty. He organized support in the Ballynure area amongst the poor Gaels. Campbell's sympathies were always with the peasants. He wrote that the afflicted poor were seldom mourned and often forgotten. He cried out to Mother Earth: "Oh, Campbell, leave your grief and pain, and quickly come away." Campbell gave 100 per cent support to the 1798 rebellion, but he was afterwards arrested by the military authorities. All the poems in his house were seized and destroyed, but those he had given to neighbours over the years remained safe.

He had to go to gaol for a while, but he was eventually released and allowed to return to his home. He was allowed to go back to his writing, and one of his latter poems is named after a man, Willie Wark, who had been caught in the rebellion. His poem about Willie said that for several summers he had seen the heather and the bells of blue, but in 1798 he had taken up arms again.

Campbell died in 1818, leaving three sons and four daughters. He was buried in an old burial ground attached to Ballynure Church. A collection of the poems and songs of James Campbell of Ballynure was published in 1870 by S. Corry, and the preface was written by John Fullerton.

There has been a long tradition in Carncastle that the grandfather of Lord Plunket, Lord Chancellor of Ireland, was at one time an inhabitant of the parish. It is thought that he was a schoolmaster there. His school was made out of stone, and the ruins of the school were still standing at the turn of the nineteenth century.

At the beginning of the eighteenth century Patrick Plunket, a native of the area, was the schoolmaster at Carncastle. There is some evidence to support the fact that this was the same Patrick Plunket who was minister at Glasslough, County Monaghan, and who was most certainly the grandfather of the 1st Baron Plunket. Records for the Synod of Ulster in 1710 show a Patrick Plunket as a probationer in the Irish Presbyterian Church. He was licensed without ministerial charge, and he was one of the few ministers who could preach in Irish. It seems likely that he would have secured a teaching position so that he would have a source of income.

The Reverend Patrick Plunket had a son who was ordained – the Reverend Thomas Plunket. He was minister at Enniskillen and, later, Dublin. He died in 1778. It was in Enniskillen that his son William Conyngham Plunket, the Lord Chancellor, was born in 1764. He went on to be a distinguished Irish lawyer, and he was responsible for prosecuting Robert Emmett, one of the rebel leaders of the 1798 rebellion. Plunket sat for many years in the Irish (and, later, the British) Parliament before being appointed to the positions of Attorney General and then Lord Chancellor. He held this position – the most important legal position – from 1830 to 1841. In 1827 he was created a British peer under the title of Lord Plunket. He died in 1854, aged ninety. He left behind him a reputation for eloquence and ability which perhaps inclines the Carncastle people to cherish the tradition that his grandfather was Patrick Plunket, who taught their forefathers at a school in Drains Bog.

One of the curiosities of Ballygally is its Old Mill. The cotton mill was established about 1813 and employed up to 100 people, old and young. Most of these were women and children. The youngest children had to work twelve and a half hours per day for one and sixpence per week. There were no local fairs or markets so the cotton had to be taken to Glenarm or Larne to be sold.

In 1833 Lieutenant Hore of Carncastle reported that the cotton industry had closed down the previous year. Owing to the high price demanded at Belfast for the raw material, the business had become unprofitable. However, Lieutenant Hore noted that the owner of the cotton mill planned to open again.

By 1835, according to the Memoirs of the Parish of Carncastle, the owner of the factory, true to his word, was in business again. However, in February of that year some persons unknown set fire to his factory, destroying most of the equipment. The two-storey building, fifty feet by eighty feet, was burned to the ground. All that remained was the waterwheel, twenty-two feet in diameter.

There were two other mills in the region. Near the cotton mill was a watermill driven by an eighteen-foot waterwheel; in the townland of Ballyruther there was a flax mill with a twelve-foot waterwheel; and near to that was a small dairy also operated by a waterwheel.

By the late nineteenth and early twentieth century the old cotton mill had been rebuilt as a corn mill – the business it had originally been built for. Water was brought down from a dam further up a small river by a long wooden sluiceway to turn a waterwheel connected to two large stone wheels within the mill. The corn was crushed between the two stone wheels. The owner of the mill at this time was Robert Aiken. Today there is no trace of the waterwheel but the Old Mill itself has changed very little in the last 100 years.

The Deer Park Creamery in the Antrim Hills was opened in 1909. A meeting had been held in 1908 to consider the possibility of establishing a creamery in the area, and it was agreed that a cooperative dairy society should be formed. The Department of Agriculture was asked to send an expert to select a site for the creamery that would best serve the entire community. Further meetings took place in Longfield school and in Dan Mulvenna's farmhouse. The general consensus was that the creamery should serve the whole area. Robert Wilson of Deer Park West agreed that the creamery could be on his land. Johnny Wilson proposed that £1 shares in the creamery be allocated for every cow that supplied milk. Instalments were set at two shillings and sixpence.

Dear Park Creamery was built in 1908 by Paddy Rowan for the sum of £250, and second-hand equipment was bought at a cost of £180 from a creamery that had just closed down in Banbridge, County Down. The first milk was supplied on 3 May 1909. The first manager was appointed at fifteen shillings per week.

At first the only people employed at the creamery were the manager and the boiler man, Dan Boyle of Drumcrow. The manager took in the milk from the farmers' carts, put it through the separator, collected samples and recorded each sample. The boiler man fixed the boiler, weighed out the skimmed milk and washed up afterwards.

James Wilson had a store at Deer Park Creamery where he kept animal feed.

After Mr Surgeoner resigned as manager in 1910, Jon McQuillan took over. He was succeeded by his cousin, Henry McQuillan, a year later. Henry married Rose McKinty of Deer Park. He left in 1922. Herbert Hyde, a Donegal man, became manager the same year. His brother, Bertie Hyde, took over in 1924. Bertie married Ellen Wilson in 1927, and a year later he resigned. Jim Baxter of Donegal took over in 1928, beginning an association with the creamery which was to last for fifty-two years. He left in 1980, but shortly afterwards Jim was persuaded to come out of retirement and step into the manager's shoes once again. His final retirement came in 1982, when Stanley Murphy of Fermanagh took over. Jim's association with the Deer Park Cooperative Creamery did not end there: in 1982 he built a bungalow opposite the creamery and continued to be involved as its secretary.

In 1909, Richard Campbell, a native of Deer Park, was appointed judge, under the judiciary of the United States, in the Philippines. He was born in 1870, the second son of Felix Campbell of Deer Park and Mary Connolly of Aughagash. Richard Campbell received the first part of his education under his father, who was the schoolmaster at Feystown. Later he attended St Malachy's College, Belfast. At seventeen years of age he emigrated to the United States, like so many of his fellow Irishman. He started life in the US as a newspaper reporter, first in New York and later in Philadelphia and Washington. President Roosevelt appointed him, in 1902, as assistant to the Attorney General of the Philippines, and he served four years in this post. Then he was appointed as district attorney of the Moro province, and he was elected a member of the legislative council. He was appointed a judge of the supreme court of America in the Philippines, and a newspaper of the time reported that Richard Campbell was a brilliant writer and an able lawyer, and that he had a thorough knowledge of Spanish and other languages. He was an authority on Spanish law and language, and his judgement was described as unique and almost unexampled by the inhabitants, both Christian and non-Christian. On many occasions he received praise from the president for his work. He was also a member of the Knights Columbus, Georgetown University Club and the Catholic Club of New York. He was secretary of the American Committee for Relief in Ireland. In October 1921 he visited Dublin with the treasurer of the committee, and he took the opportunity of visiting his family in Deer Park.

When he arrived at Glenarm a large Gaelic athletic event was held. A match between the Cushendall Pearses and a Glenarm team took place, and many notable people took up the challenge. Judge Campbell was thinking of visiting Northern Ireland again in 1935, but he died at his home in New York before he could make the trip. He was one of nine children.

His sisters, Rosetta, Maggie and Jane, moved to Larne where Rosetta opened a small restaurant at 47 Pound Street in the early part of the century.

The Catholic church was built on the lower part of the Carncastle road in 1944, and this was a big step forward for Ballygally, a mainly Protestant community. The church was dedicated to St Joseph on Sunday 14 May by the Most Reverend Dr Mageean, Bishop of Down and Connor. Before this, the parishioners had to travel to Glenarm to attend a church, or they walked on the rough road over the Ballygilbert Hill to Feystown.

Catholicism came to Ireland with the arrival of St Patrick in about AD 432. He had come from Rome, where Pope Celestine I had exhorted him to return to Ireland and establish Christianity there. He was enslaved at Slemish for about six years, but somehow he managed to escape, probably travelling down the Antrim Hills to the region of Ballygally and Larne on his way to Scotland, where it is almost certain that he originated, being brought up as a Christian in the latter days of the Roman Empire in Britain. Slemish is about ten miles from Ballygally.

St Joseph's is quite small, but it would have cost a lot of money to build. It is situated in what must have been a field.

I passed the church many times in my walks in the hills, and at eighteen years of age I became curious about the beliefs of the Roman Catholic Church. I travelled to Belfast on my moped to seek out books on the Church and other subjects. There is an atmosphere of papacy in the Antrim Hills around Ballygally, and, looking across the North Channel to Scotland, I imagined the early Christians coming to Ulster in their little boats from the Roman Empire, which was then in sharp decline. St Patrick's, Carncastle (Church of Ireland) is bigger than St Joseph's, and they have much in common as far as doctrine and dogmas are concerned. St Joseph's is, however, totally Rome-orientated. The Pope's ex-cathedra pronouncements about beliefs are considered to be infallible. The Catholic Church in the Carncastle region has been tolerated by Protestants, and in the Troubles there have been no incidents.

In the Mass the priest turns wine into the blood of Christ and bread into His body – a doctrine not subscribed to by the Protestant communities. Upon entering the church, Catholics bow before the image of the Blessed Virgin Mary – a central person in worship – but the person of Christ is of course of much more importance. Modern Roman Catholicism appears to be more Bible-based than in previous ages, but the decisions of the Pope are held to be more important than the decisions of the Church councils. The present Pope is Benedict XVI.

I think it is true to say that Roman Catholics have a firmer system of beliefs than Protestants. Liberal ideas are more accepted in the non-Roman communions, and traditional faith has been eroded. In contrast, throughout the ages little churches like St Joseph's have held fast to the ancient Catholic beliefs, and they continue to pride themselves on their infallible Pope.

All denominations claim that they are right, and modern youth may still believe in God – the Author of the Universe who became man to save the world.

St Joseph's is about a five-minute walk from the Church of Ireland rectory, and the modern primary school lies only a few minutes' walk from the Church of Ireland rectory, and is open to all classes and creeds. The school was formerly in a small building situated near the churches of the Presbyterian and Unitarian faiths at Carncastle.

The Annals refer to one of the churches at Tullagh, which the Reverend O'Laverty believes to be situated in the townland in Carncastle. He points out that there was a graveyard there containing the ruins of a church measuring forty-eight feet by forty feet. St Cunning is referred to in the Calendar of Donegal in September as 'Conaing, son of Lucunan, a saint'. According to a report of the Parliamentary Commission, an inquest held at Antrim town on 23 October 1637 recorded that St Cunning had 'no church, glebe, nor incumbent'. Although the church was not in use, some of the walls were still standing, for in 1833 Lieutenant Thomas Hore reported that there was no Roman Catholic chapel but there were the ruins of one in the buildings of St Cunning. Today the ruins of the church are barely visible in a field called Church Park, belonging to James Hunter. David Mulvenna of Ballygowan is the owner of a font said to have belonged to the church.

There was also a church at Solar. This ancient parish extends over Minnis (North and South), Slievebane, Drumnagreagh, Solar and Lisnahay (North and South). The church measured forty-eight feet by twenty feet, and dated from after the death of St Patrick. In 1268 two parts of the land in Solar were let by Robert le Fleming, Bishop of Connor, to John Bisset of Glenarm. By 1622 the church had fallen into decay, and the lands of Solar, still in the Bishop's hands, were let to the Earls of Antrim. In the Antrim Inquisition of 1657, a small rectory at Solar was described as belonging to the Bishop of Down. There was no church or glebe. Patrick Adair, a noted preacher, served in the parish at this time.

In the late nineteenth century in the Belfast Museum stood an ancient bell known as the Bell of Solar. It was presented by James Boyle. The bell was cast out of sheet iron coated in molten bronze.

A few years ago Stephen Brady, a local farmer, was ploughing a field when he unearthed a quantity of bones, and it is believed that the field could be the site of a graveyard attached to the church at Solar.

A 'headless cross' used to stand on a hillside near the townland borders of Linford and Drains Bog at a pass leading to Carncastle. The cross disappeared many years ago. History gives us no clues as to why the cross was erected, but O'Laverty suggests that it could be where warriors had died defending the pass. The place was also marked by a succession of cairns, built or repaired until as late as the sixteenth century. In the late nineteenth and early twentieth centuries the stone cairns were removed, and marks seem to have been transferred to a large basalt boulder, standing six feet high, situated nearby. It has been suggested that a low, circular stone construction like the one at Cashel lay at the pass on the main Deer Park to Carncastle road. Perhaps the remains of this construction, resembling a cairn, was called a 'headless cross'.

The Normans reached the Carncastle area shortly after their initial invasion of Ireland in 1169. They had marched north from the Waterford area with an impressive retinue to subdue the Gaels of both the north and the south of the country. The Pope gave his blessing to this enterprise, and Henry II of England arrived in the Emerald Isle with his troops.

The Normans under William the Conqueror had invaded England in 1066, and they had defeated Harold II at the Battle of Hastings. It is not clear if at this time William had an invasion of Ireland in view, but certainly he regarded Ireland as a hostile nation. Over a century later the Normans set foot in Ireland. However, the invasion of Ireland was not undertaken with the same enthusiasm as that of England, for Ireland was a much poorer realm. The invasion was made difficult by the fact that the country was divided into about 150 tribal kingdoms, and each one had to be conquered individually.

The High King of Tara resided some miles north of Dublin in the valley of the River Boyne. He failed to unite Ireland, even though the country was threatened with submergence by the Normans, the most powerful race in Europe. The Normans, however, were only able to conquer a minority of the *tuatha*, or tribal kingdoms. There was chaos on both sides. Ulster was remote, situated in the north-east of Ireland, and Ulster held out longer than the other Gaelic kingdoms.

The Normans eventually resigned themselves to ruling only the present-day counties of Antrim and Down. They called the new kingdom Ulidia, or Ulster. They probed up the Antrim coast, building mottes (small fortifications) by means of which they hoped to control the natives.

John de Courcy, who was made 1st Earl of Ulster by King John, conquered the area of Laharna, or Larne, at the start of the present-day coast road. He was, however, defeated by O'Flynn, the king of Uí Tuirtre in 1178. De Courcy was wounded in this battle. The kingdom maintained its independence under the O'Flynn kings until the late fourteenth century. Uí Tuirtre covered the north-western half of County Antrim from Glenarm to the River Bann, and as far south as Lough Neagh, or the Great Lake. The area of Laharna seems to have been at first well settled by the Normans.

After King John had granted the lands around Ballygally, Drains Bay and Carncastle to the Norse-Gaelic family that ruled Galloway in Scotland, they became known as the Galloways or Fitzgilberts. Their control of the area appears to have been effective, for, according to a valuation held in the Glens in 1276, it was by far the most prosperous area in the region.

There was a mill at Droagh, near Ballygally, and another one along with a castle at Carncastle. The only other mill in the entire region was the one at Glenarm.

A motte was built at Carncastle, from where the whole area from Ballygally to Drains Bay was patrolled. The builder was perhaps the Norman knight called Richard Hackett, whose name lives on in the townland of Ballyhackett (Carncastle).

Another motte was built at Milltown. In recent years a stream was diverted to drive watermills here – hence the name Milltown. There were at least six watermills here in the nineteenth century.

Inland from Ballygally, over the winding roads with spectacular views, we reach Carnalbanagh ('the cairn of the Scotsmen'). After the Battle of Pathfoot, the Scots made for Slemish with the intention of attacking the town of Connor. The Scots are reported to have erected large cairns to commemorate their great march. One of the cairns gave its name to Carnave, a townland outside Glenarm village, at the first of the Glens. Another gave its name to Carnalbanagh. It was here, according to tradition, that another battle was fought with the McQuillans, and the Scots were again in the ascendant. The cairn at Carnalbanagh must have been erected to commemorate some important event, for its magnitude in the early nineteenth century was said to be breathtaking. Today there are no remains of the cairn to be seen.

In 1859 there was a great religious revival in Ulster, and this was particularly evident at Carnalbanagh. Church attendances increased, and the number of people taking Holy Communion grew. The meeting house at Carnalbanagh was for all denominations, and moves were made to build a new church. In 1862, 107 families from Glenarm, Carncastle, Carnalbanagh and Buckna signed a petition and promised a stipend of £33 12s 6d for the support of the minister.

It transpired that the Earl of Antrim was unable to give a lease to the General Assembly for interdenominational prayer at the meeting house. A public meeting was held in November 1862, and the Carnalbanagh people through their representatives and others said that they would build a new place of worship. A list of stipend-payers was presented, and the Presbytery asked for a site for the new church. Lord Antrim donated two acres of land in 1863 for the site of the church and a manse. The meeting house was, of course, interdenominational and it was later converted into a national schoolhouse under the Earl's patronage. The old schoolhouse was used as temporary accommodation for the congregation.

Laharna Hotel, Larne.

Chapter 1

Glenarm

There are nine glens of Antrim: Glenarm ('the glen of the armed force'); Glencloy ('the glen of the dykes'); Glenariff ('The glen of the plough'); Glenballyeamon ('the glen of Edward's town'); Glenaan ('the blue glen', or 'the glen of the proverb', or 'the little glen'); Glencorp ('the glen of the corpses'); Glendun ('the glen of the brown river'); Glenshesk ('the glen of the sedges'); and Glentaisie ('the glen of the princess').

Of all the glens of the Antrim coast, Glenarm stands out for it boasts green hills and a blue bay and a shining quay. There are bright birds and flowers in sunny bowers. The sweet river flows free. Strange legends surround the glen, so long untold, and there were fair scenes of festive glee. There was a spire, where ancient ivy climbed the church amidst bowering trees, and there was a tower from which bells peeled the evening chimes. There was a flag that flouted the breeze. There was a chapel, a courthouse, a fountain, a mill, a school by Castle Bridge, houses clustered up the hill, and planting on the ridge. Here in Glenarm, Scotia's earliest settlers stood on Erin's emerald strand.

The Bissets were blamed for Athol's blood, and, with feigned crusading band, made the glens of Antrim their holy land. They spread along the shore until Margery, last of the line of Bisset, married Mor MacDonnell.

From here the Earls of Antrim sprung, who built the grey castle, where great deeds were seen and sung. There were round ivy towers, in parks and bowers, filled with doves and pheasants gay. The hare and deer sport safely here, and the trout and salmon play.

In the early sixties, I was a pupil at Larne Grammar School, and on Sundays I would make ready to drive up the Antrim coast road with my parents. My mother always prepared a flask of hot dark tea and she would provide us with cheese and tomato sandwiches. There were also digestive biscuits that cost the vast sum of one and sixpence. My father had a Ford Zodiac, which he had bought from a garage in Ballymena for about £500 – a great sum in those days.

My father held the important position of the County Dental Officer, and his headquarters were in Alexandra Gardens off the Antrim Road in Belfast.

I was in my early teens and my brother Derek had just gained admission to Queens University Belfast. At Larne Grammar School I had started to realize that I lived in a most beautiful part of the world, for the Antrim coast and the Glens of Antrim are one of the great beauty spots in these islands – and, indeed, the world! The Glens stretch on to the Causeway Coast and, of course, the Giant's Causeway.

My mother and father often went on outings on Saturdays but the extended full-day trips were usually on a Sunday.

My Uncle Jim had died in 1957, and my mother and father came to live in the bungalow at Ballygally in 1955 to look after him in his old age. Formerly we had lived at Finaghy, just outside Belfast. I have even earlier memories of living in Drumderg, Draperstown. I remember an old country house, and walking up a lane to it. Before this my parents lived in England, where I was born at St Neots, Huntingdonshire. My Uncle Jim was from County Down, and so were both my parents. My father was born in Newry, and my mother in Rathmullen. I have early memories of Rathmullen and the farm that she grew up in.

Ballygally was a complete contrast to Finaghy. I was enchanted by the greens of the countryside, the haystacks in the fields and the sheep and cattle. I would climb Ballygally Head, where there was a striking view of Scotland and the Mull of Kintyre. I imagined early man making the journey across the North Channel in their curraghs and coming ashore on the beach at Ballygally Bay. Ballygally means 'townland of the rocks', and in olden days there may not have been sand at Ballygally. The view across from the strand is entirely of rocks. I remember my mother leading me by the hand along the coast, and I particularly remember an old boat of about twenty feet that lay on the rocks in an inlet.

My father was a keen photographer. He took many pictures of the Antrim coast and the Glens, but these alas! have been lost. I had a little cine camera that he bought me in Larne for £15 as well as a movie projector, and I would make films about the scenery of the Antrim coast. The little camera could make a four-minute film at one go. After a while my father bought a Bolex 8-mm camera for £100 in Belfast; it could make a fifteen-minute film at one go. The films are now with my brother Derek in England, and he also has films of him and his wife, Helen, before they were married.

Colour for 8-mm movies was in its infancy, and a reel of colour film cost a guinea. My father also took photographs of the garden of our bungalow, which was full of roses that he bought from MacGreedy's, outside Belfast.

Glenarm has a population of about 1,000. There is a bank and a police station in the village. Glenarm is the seat of the MacDonnell clan. They live in a large house, which is approached via Castle Street in the village.

The town itself dates back to the reign of King John; it is mentioned that in 1210 the King granted the townland a charter. It is perhaps the oldest town in Ireland, and in the reign of King John a castle was built there.

Many varieties of flowers spring up in the Glens, and they are a joy to see. As a child I did not know their names, but I was enchanted by their sweet perfumes. Each season brought something new. At Larne Grammar School we were taken for nature study up the Lower Cairncastle Road. I kept a little scrapbook, and I pressed flowers and stuck them into it.

I started at the prep school attached to Larne Grammar School when I was about eight years of age, having previously been at Finaghy Primary School.

Both my mother and my father were great lovers of plants, and I refer the reader back to the many varieties of roses my father grew in our garden. The slopes along the coast, as one travels towards Glenarm, are studded with primroses in the spring; wild hyacinths and early purple orchids abound.

There is an impressive view of Glenarm and McAuley's Head from Ballygally.

The headlands, with their valleys and fields, come alive with all sorts of vegetation. There are three headlands that jut out into the North Channel and they all enchant the traveller. There is a regular bus service from Larne.

According to some authorities, some of the plants found in the Glenarm area are more characteristic of North Britain – the wood cranesbill, the wood cow wheat, the tea-leaved willow and the few-flowered sedge. On the plateau near Garron grew two sedges unknown elsewhere in Ireland, and there can also be found the rare yellow marsh saxifrage. As a child I loved the primroses that fluttered in the wind, and I often thought of writing poetry about them – I had a little poem about snowdrops published in the school magazine when I was about ten, but alas! it has been forgotten. As a child I knew that after the primroses came the bright roses, white, pink and red, and the giant fairy thimbles. I loved the little yellow flowers that dotted the moorland that I loved; and fuchsia hedges waved above me, reminding me of fairy lanterns. Then came the purple heather, the gold of bracken, the bright berry-laden rowans and haws, and the blaze of holly set in rich emerald. The smell of honeysuckle lit up my childhood summers. The long-stemmed buttercups were warm-clutched flowers for the jam jar in our small kitchen.

Glenarm is a privately owned glen on the estate of the Earl of Antrim, who lives in a large country house only a short walk from Glenarm. The castle, set amongst woods, has been the residence of the MacDonnells of Antrim since 1636. An inscription over the entrance to the castle states that with the leave of God the castle was built by Randal MacDonnell, knight, Earl of Antrim. The castle it is more like a country house than a castle.

I visited Glenarm Castle in 1990 with a group from Gloucester Park Day Centre, along with my friend Hilary Alexander. Here we met Lady Flora MacDonnell, who spoke with a cultivated English accent. We travelled by minibus along the coast road from Larne, passing through those interesting places described earlier in this book. Hilary befriended Lady Flora, and she managed to obtain an art studio in the barbican of the castle.

Glenarm is well wooded, with a brown, stony river spanned by attractive old bridges. There is also a deer park. Richard Dobbs in his

Description of the County of Antrim (1683) wrote that above Glenarm was a glen through which a river flowed, and it was clad with underwoods. They were the most pleasant hunting grounds he had ever seen: 'One might have the dogs or bucks continually in view.'

As a child at Larne Grammar School I did not know much about the MacDonnells of Antrim, but my mother would sometimes talk about these rich people and the land they owned in the Antrim Hills and on the coast. I learned that poachers took fish from the river there; the Earl of Antrim often spoke out against them.

In the deer park the Girl Guides and others set up camp, their fires crackling, with the hope of no rain. It was here that Maureen Donnelly, author of *The Nine Glens*, used to camp; and it was here that her grandfather, Richard McFetridge, lived as a boy before he and his brother, William John, settled in the Cushendall area. The McFetridges, a sub-clan of the O'Bresslans of Donegal, has for a long time been associated with the MacDonnells of the Glens of Antrim. In an old account of a battle at Dunluce Castle, further up the coast in 1641, one Captain McPhedris is said to have given warning that Dunluce, a MacDonnell stronghold, was about to be attacked by the O'Neills. McPedris meant 'son of Peter', and over the years the name has been corrupted to McPhedris. Many people of this name still live in the Glens.

Near the castle can be seen the remains of the old church of Templeoughter.

In the townland of Solar, nearby, was another old church, the bell of which, made from thin sheet iron, is in the Ulster Museum. It is at Glenarm that Shane O'Neill is supposed to have been buried after his killing by the MacDonnells at Cushendun, as mentioned previously.

A holy friar came from Armagh to the Abbot of Glenarm, and he said, "Father, I have come from our brothers of Armagh to ask you if it is all right to remove the body of the great O'Neill for the purpose of burial in the tomb of his ancestors at Armagh."

The Abbot of Glenarm paused for a moment before answering. He asked if he had brought with him the remains of James MacDonnell, Lord of Antrim and Kintyre, who was buried at Armagh.

The friar answered that he had not brought the wished-for remains.

The Abbot replied, "Whilst you continue to tread on the grave of James, Lord of Antrim and Kintyre, we in Glenarm will continue to trample on the dust of the great O'Neill."

Just beyond Glenarm, on the seaward side of the coast road, is an opening in the white rocks where ancient man would have peered out to the North Channel. It has been called the Madman's Window. It gets its name from a legend that someone committed suicide in the area. Not far away on a slope is Straidkilly, the slipping village. Inch by inch this eerie deserted village moves slowly towards the sea. I can remember my mother pointing out the Madman's Window to me, although she did not mention anything about a suicide. Perhaps in the age of the Early Church, solitary monks would look through the gap, praying to God. Solitary holy men are common to many regions of Christianity, especially in the latter days of the Roman Empire.

The Romans, of course, did not conquer Ireland, but Roman generals must have stood on the Mull of Kintyre making plans for conquest. Glenarm, being by the sea, would have been an easy target for them, and its inhabitants must have lived in constant fear of an invasion by the cruel and resourceful Romans.

Glenarm in modern times is a compact community, nestling at the end of the glen, sheltered by a massive limestone cliff. It straddles the dark-brown peat-stained river and is situated on the curve of the bay. The headlands, as at Ballygally, can be seen, and a church spire stands out. There is an abundance of trees, and one can take interesting walks. It takes about fifteen or twenty minutes to walk from the harbour at Glenarm to the end of the village, and everywhere there is the atmosphere of the sea.

However, the beauty of Glenarm has been spoilt by dust produced by the quarries which operate above the village. Here limestone is crushed to produce a powdered lime, for use in agriculture, and whiting for the paint trade. Much of the life of Glenarm revolves around its castle, and the Earls of Antrim were generally well beloved in the region.

The barbican of Glenarm Castle, with its bridge, looks like something out of Grimm's fairy tales. In more turbulent times the barbican had its own drawbridge. There is a grim reminder of those hostile times, for there are seven murder-holes for pouring boiling oil on intruders from the roof of the archway.

The gateway was built and the castle restored by Edmund MacDonnell and his wife, Anne Catherine, in 1825. Anne was, in her own right, Countess of Antrim and Viscountess Dunluce.

There was a castle at Glenarm long before the present structure. The original castle was built by the Bissets about 1255, and this family acquired the Glens of Antrim by the marriage of John Mor MacDonnell with Margery Bisset in 1399. The castle was rebuilt in 1603, renovated by Alexander MacDonnell in 1756 and renovated again by Anne Catherine MacDonnell in 1791. In 1929 it was gutted by fire and rebuilt yet another time.

The present Earls of Antrim, like other Irish peers, cannot sit in the House of Lords in Britain.

The MacDonnells are one of the most ancient families in Ireland; they can trace their origins back to the thirteenth century.

As a child I was only dimly aware that Antrim boasted aristocracy, and on our trips down the coast my mother and father did not drive up Castle Street; nor do I have it on any of my old 8-mm home movies. Certainly the presence of the Earls of Antrim adds colour to the Glens, and to Ulster.

The original Earl of Antrim came across the North Channel and settled in the Glens to cause trouble for Elizabeth I in the sixteenth century.

The town boasts two main churches. The parish church of Glenarm was built by Alexander MacDonnell, Earl of Antrim, in 1763. It was erected on the site of the Franciscan abbey, founded in 1463 by Robert Bisset. The church is attractively situated amongst some trees, and its spire is visible for miles. The church is quite small, but it served as a place of worship for both the aristocracy and the common people. It is similar to the church at Ballycastle, in that there are round portholes in the spire. Some stone remains from the old abbey are preserved in the church.

The second church is the church of the Immaculate Conception. Prior to 1865 the Catholics of Glenarm attended Mass in a barn at the rear of a house owned by Mary O'Neill, in Altmore Street. The church has only a small spire, and it is about the same size as the parish church of Glenarm. The site of the church was purchased from Robert Gibson and the building was designed by O'Neill & Byrne, architects, of Belfast. The building contractor was a local firm. It was named in an advertisement in Bassett's *County Antrim* (1886) as Baker & Groser.

Thus were the two faiths represented in the village: the Church of Ireland in the parish church and Roman Catholics in the Church of the Immaculate Conception. There was little or no sectarian strife in the area, and even during the Troubles the two religions worshipped in peace. However, the Protestants had no liking for the Pope, and the Catholics had no liking for Protestant England, which had dominated all of Ireland and brought the Scots to the Glens.

Toberwine Street, meaning the sweet or pure well, is one of Glenarm's main thoroughfares. There were two main hotels – Darragh's Commercial Hotel and the Antrim Arms Hotel; the owner of the Antrim Arms Hotel in 1913 was John Clarke, a local historian and writer. He published a number of books under the nom de plume of Benmore. Next door to the hotel was the barracks of the Royal Irish Constabulary (now the Police Service of Northern Ireland), which later became part of the hotel.

Prior to the building of the coast road in the 1830s, small trading ships were able to anchor at high water near the warehouses at the back of Toberwine Street. From here, some loads, such as limestone and iron, were fed down chutes directly into the ships' holds. However, the water was normally too low, so large vessels had to anchor in deep water in the bay and lighters carried freight out to them.

A small harbour and pier have existed at Glenarm since the fifteenth century. The pier, together with eight acres (Irish) of the surrounding land were owned by the Bisset family. The Bissets' land extended to the Franciscan abbey. The pier was the only one along the coast from Larne to Ballycastle, and it was here that material was landed for the building of Glenarm Castle.

Another pier was built here in 1864 by a Mr Hanbury under a Crown lease. It was enlarged and improved in 1868 by William Reid of Magheramorne. The Crown lease expired in November 1898, at the same time as the lease for the quarries nearby. The Commissioner of Woods sold the pier to Lord Antrim, then owner of the quarries.

There was an increase of traffic through Glenarm in the late nineteenth century, due to the export of iron ore and limestone. The harbour was further improved in 1910.

Most of the ships in those days were schooners, crewed by three men and one boy and owned by local businessmen, but steam-driven ships were becoming more fashionable. During the First World War the schooners ceased to be used locally.

In an article in the *Glenarm Journal* in 1980 Alex Maguire of Straidkilly Road, Glenarm, wrote about the harbour in the early years of the twentieth century. He described ships loaded up with timber right up to the coast-road bridge opposite St Patrick's Church. The first quay for loading iron ore was further down the river on the same side, but later another iron-ore quay was built opposite the mill. One Billy Bunting of Glenarm recalled five small ships in the harbour waiting to load up with limestone for export, while another lay at anchor in the bay waiting to enter the harbour.

Glenarm lies in a beautiful wooded valley. An old black-and-white photograph of it shows the headland with its limestone cliffs. Along the seashore are houses, and in the background are the Antrim Hills. It is a pity that the village has been marred by the limestone quarries.

Glenarm Village.

The slipe, or wheelless slide car, was a common mode of transport in the Glens in the days before proper roads. This primitive-looking vehicle was simply two shafts fastened together with a pair of *slotes*, or crosspieces, to carry a load. It was ideal, for it could be drawn by horse or pony over rough or marshy ground where a wheeled vehicle would become bogged down. It was used for transporting corn. An old black-and-white photograph shows a slipe drawn by a Cushendall pony. In the background is a peasant's thatched cottage. Two men can be seen at work. Cottages like this were common in the Antrim Hills and the Glenarm area.

Chapter 2

Glencloy

This beautiful glen reaches the sea at Carnlough, a short distance from Glenarm. It is a favourite spot for photographers, and it is featured in some of my 8-mm movies. The harbour in the village stands out, like that of Glenarm. It has been painted many times. It is a wonder how the ships manoeuvre into the harbour, which is situated in the centre of the village.

Like Glenarm, Glencloy has white chalk quarries, so ships loaded up here.

Patchwork fields surround Carnlough, and on the road to the village there is also a caravan site, which in the summer is full of tourists. The fields are neatly bounded by stone dykes that give Glencloy its name. The glen has also been called Glencule.

The Carnlough low-back car was a development from the slipe. The body of the cart was fastened on horizontally. Old photographs show that Cushendall ponies were used. The Glens of Antrim was one of the last areas in Ulster to abandon the low-back car, with its solid wooden wheels.

Cranny Falls are situated near Carnlough in a deep, wooded glen. There is a lovely walk along the quiet riverbank. A doonan (little fort) was close to the village, situated on the east side of the Doonan River, a tributary of the Glencloy River.

Upon entering Carnlough in my father's car, our first stop was always for an ice cream.

Carnlough lies at the foot of Glencloy, the shallowest of the Glens, and the town surrounds an impressive beach. Near the glen are the

Carnlough Harbour.

Carnlough and Bay from Creggan.

Sheddings on the Ballymena road, where there is a cluster of houses called Cashel. Cashel is built on the ruins of a very old Celtic settlement. Ticloy Hill, two miles (3 km) north of Cashel, has a portal grave near the summit. The region has a long farming history, and the exceptional neatness of the drystone walls makes patterns on the hillsides. Doonan Waterfall, on the Glencloy River, is near Doonan Fort, two and a half miles (4 km) above Carnlough.

The central attraction of Carnlough is the limestone bridge over the main street. It was built by Lord and Lady Londonderry in 1854 to carry the little railway that brought limestone from the quarries to the harbour. An inscription, however, says that it was built to commemorate the landing of Frances Anne Vane, Lady Londonderry, on her pier.

Beside the harbour is a clock tower, the former town hall and the harbour office, which was built with great blocks of limestone.

The harbour is now mainly used by pleasure boats, though lobster, crab and salmon fishing are carried on.

Near the harbour is the famous Londonderry Arms Hotel, which still has the atmosphere of a Georgian coaching inn. Carnlough has a number of other interesting pubs, with great charm.

The Carnlough River tumbles down a small glen of its own, not included amongst the nine glens of Antrim. The visitor should venture up Waterfall Road to see, first, an ancient lime kiln. This has been described by the Heritage Society as a noble monument of industrial archaeology. It has tall, white chimneys. Higher up lies the Cranny Falls, as mentioned. This stretch of the river is frequented by dippers and wagtails. Higher still by a track there is the start of the great Garron moorland, where lapwing, curlew, snipe and rarer birds can be found.

The village holds a festival in July, over the space of a fortnight.

Carnlough was the home of George Shields, author of *The New Gossoon*, and many other Gaelic kitchen comedies. Their popularity is undiminished.

There is a resident violin-maker. On the Doonan River, two and a half miles (4 km) along the Ballymena road, attractive printed textiles are produced.

During the Troubles, Carnlough and its glen were havens for those who wanted to avoid the strife in Belfast and other nearby regions. People had started to visit the Antrim coast, especially

Ballygally, in the mid-sixties, at a time when there was a start to prosperity. Cars would be parked along the seafront on Sundays, and this was a time when few local people had cars. A modern car park has been built at Ballygally where once there were open fields and a tennis court.

At the turn of the twentieth century, Carnlough boasted a lime-processing industry. Limestone was burned here before being shipped to Glasgow for the munitions factories. Old photographs show the large lead-lined retorts in which peat from the mountain above the village was burned with sulphuric acid in the manufacture of sulphate ammonia. The product was shipped from Carnlough Harbour.

The bus from Larne to Cushendall wends its way along the coast road. It affords a great view of the headlands and the sea, all for a moderate price.

When we made the journey by car, my father would often stop for a flask of tea with some biscuits, and we would spread a rug on the grass. This was in an age when there was little traffic on the road. The ice creams we used to have in Carnlough were made by Ulster Creameries, not Dale Farm or other less well-known makers. I often made films of the sea and coast with my cine camera when we made stops. I have about two hours or more of cine film, and in those days I would show it in the front room of my parents' little bungalow at Ballygally. The film was sent off to England for processing, and it returned about a week later – a beautiful length of film manufactured by Kodak. I was in the process of learning about the Antrim coast and hills. Their history was gleaned from my parents. My father had some interest in Irish history, but alas! he was a Liberal Unionist.

At that time there was a ceasefire in Northern Ireland, and it was wonderful to be able to make our way up the coast without fear of trouble; unfortunately this was not to last very long.

The end of my schooling was spent at Orange's Academy, and here too, near the end of the sixties, there was little trouble. However, the *Protestant Telegraph* was making its appearance. I watched the Reverend Ian Paisley on television, but no one thought that Ulster would descend into the horrors of the late sixties and seventies. However, the Antrim coast avoided the worst of the Troubles.

Hamill's Hotel was established in 1857, selling alcohol. It had painted, imitation stonework. Many years later it catered mainly for cyclists. Outside there was an ornamental drinking trough for horses. In the background of a black-and-white photograph, dated about 1912, stands the clock tower and of course the limestone railway bridge. At that time there was even less traffic on the road.

A long-car took tourists from the Londonderry Arms Hotel to view the coast.

The Londonderry Arms Hotel was built by Lady Londonderry in 1848. A sign on the back of the car read 'Cushendall & Ballycastle Tourist Car'. An inscription on the arch above the doors of the hotel read 'Projected and commissioned by Charles Stewart Vane, Marquis of Londonderry and completed by Frances Anne Vane, Marchioness of Londonderry, 1854'.

The harbour at Carnlough was the brainchild of Lord and Lady Londonderry in the middle of the nineteenth century. Their main residence was in County Durham, England. The harbour was needed as a result of the extensive trade in limestone. A brass plaque in the Londonderry Arms Hotel reads; 'To commemorate the landing for the first time of Frances Anne Vane, Marchioness of Londonderry, on her own pier at Carnlough Harbour on 20th August 1855'. Patrick Mahon was the stonemason who built the harbour and its arches.

As a teenager I realized the harbour was the most important feature of Carnlough, so I went to work with my cine camera again. It is not clear whether there was a landing stage at Carnlough before the building of the harbour.

The journey to Scotland in the middle of the nineteenth century would have taken several hours, depending upon the wind. Early black-and-white photographs show the harbour with one or two ships at berth.

Another attraction is the Drumnasole Waterfall to the north of Carnlough. It can be approached by a path named the Goat's Parlour. At the bottom of this path is Tubberdoney, a well that was believed to cure afflictions of the eye. Drumnasole is situated in another pretty glen two and a half miles (3 km) north of Carnlough.

In this glen nestled Drumnasole House, a great basalt building built in 1840 by Francis Turnly, the son of a Belfast brewer. He added to his father's fortune by trading with China, and upon coming home he endowed the Antrim coast with a number of architectural curiosities, including the Red Arch at Waterfoot and the gaol at Cushendall. He also built a school at Drumnasole, now disused.

On the headland of Drumnasole the Antrim Scots lit beacons to signal to their fellow Scots across the North Channel. Drumnasole means 'the ridge of light'. Dungallon Fort, nearby, is said to have been the last fort in Ireland to be held by the Vikings. Drumnasole Waterfall is perhaps overshadowed by the more dramatic falls at Glenariff, the third glen, which lies about half a mile up the coast road. A house there was built about 1819 by Francis Turnly, who was the landlord of Cushendall. Some of his descendants still live there.

Along the coast, near Carnlough, is Garron Tower, built by the Londonderry family. The Marchioness inherited the Carnlough estate in 1834. She was living in England at the time, but she wanted a residence in County Antrim. Garron Tower was the result of her longings. She chose Charles Campbell from Newtownards to build the house; he had worked for the Marquis at Mount Stewart in County Down. The foundation stone was laid by the Marchioness herself on 24 February 1848. The first stage of the work was completed in July 1849. Garron Tower is reached by an inland loop road, and it was modelled on a castle on the Rhine in Germany.

The castle is now a school – St MacNissi's College.

At home in Ballygally I would sometimes watch the bus carrying the schoolchildren from Larne to Garron Tower, and I was aware that the school was a Roman Catholic college. It is one of the best schools in Northern Ireland, ranking with the Royal Schools and the Belfast Royal Academical Institution. Ballygally was mainly a Protestant village, and its people were aware that there was a school in opposition some miles down the coast road. It is beautifully situated on a landslip shelf on the side of Garron Point.

There were two phases to the building of Garron Tower, and during the second phase the Marchioness of Londonderry made some additions to the house: alterations were made to the lodge, the porch, the ice house, the orchard house, the stable and the winery. She was accused of being extravagant at a time when Ulster was in the grip of famine, but it should be mentioned that she was responsible for many improvements in the Carnlough area, including the opening of Carnlough Literary and Philosophical Society (with its library and reading room), a temperance society and a savings bank.

The tower was opened as a hotel by Henry McNeill of Larne in 1900. During the Second World War the residents of Clifton House, Belfast, were evacuated to Garron Tower. In 1951 it was formed into a school.

Possibly Lady Londonderry wanted her tower to rival the MacDonnell castle at Glenarm. She made an inscription, which says that she hoped to live in the affections of a devoted and loyal tenantry.

While famine was still widespread in Ireland, Garron Tower underwent much improvement. The interior has fine wood carvings and may be visited by appointment. In the grounds stands the oldest eucalyptus tree in Ulster – 120 years old.

On the summit of Garron Point is Dunmaul, an ancient earth fort. Tradition states that here Vikings collected 'tribute of blackmail' from the Gaels. Here, too, is the Goat's Parlour, a favourite grazing place for wild goats.

At the foot of the cliffs below Garron Tower, beside the car park, is a small harbour the size of a swimming pool – another of the works of the Marchioness. At this harbour a succession of landslips have left the cliffs looking like a sliced sandwich cake.

Near Garron Point one of Ireland's smallest rivers, a mere five miles (8 km) in length, issues from the base of the limestone cliffs. The old Foaran Path can still be seen, and this was the main route over the point before the coast road was built. There is an old coach house, where trace horses used on the steep path were stabled. At the bend in the road, on a tablet set in the vertical face of a great limestone rock, Lady Londonderry's feelings are recorded in verse.

Just beyond the coast road stands the unusual limestone statue of the White Lady, one of the sea's most lifelike chalk carvings. Near the White Lady a lane winds up to Galboly, a deserted hamlet in lovely surroundings, overhung by alp-like crags. Until recently it had a solitary bachelor inhabitant.

To commemorate the famine years in the mid-nineteenth century, Lady Londonderry caused to be erected for the tenants a large block of limestone, which is usually referred to as the Famine Stone. Lady Londonderry was on a visit to Garron Tower during the second week of December 1848 when she instructed her agent, John Langtree, to have the inscription carved on it for her. It was her wish that the stone should be 'an imperishable memorial of Ireland's affliction and England's generosity' in the famine years, which she said were 'unparalleled in the annals of human suffering'.

Fallowvee, less than a mile from the White Lady, has an old quay from which limestone from the quarry above was shipped. A great storm in 1904 partly destroyed the quay. Ardclinis ruined church is just over a mile (2 km) from Fallowvee towards Red Bay. Until about 1760 an ancient crozier or pastoral staff rested on the ruined chancel window there. It is thought that it belonged to St Oengus MacNissi, who is said to have been the founder of the monastic see of Connor, in AD 606. The crozier was perhaps used for the administration of oaths. It is now known as the Ardclinis Crozier. It was originally about three feet two inches long, made of Irish oak protected by a covering of bronze. The bronze head was overlaid with thin silver plates. A representation of the Crucifixion was riveted on the staff, and an outline of a sheep's head among trefoils was another of its ornamentations. St Oengus MacNissi is believed to have founded the church at Ardclinis, and also to have been buried there. The boys' college at Garron Tower bears the name of this saint.

O'Laverty, who saw the crozier, says that in about 1860 the crozier was in the possession of a farmer living in the mountains above Glenarm. He is said to have dipped it into water to help sick cows, and it had been in the farmer's possession for several generations. The present home of the Ardclinis Crozier is in the National Museum of Ireland in Dublin. The Reverend Father Kevin Donnelly, once curate of Glenarm, said that a certain bishop who had to flee left the crozier in the care of the Galvin family of Glendun. He wanted them to keep it in case he did not return. The crozier was never reclaimed; it was handed down as an heirloom. The Galvin family came to live at Croc-an-dhu near Glenarm and one of the family married into the Magill Mor family. One of the Magills, Mrs Eily McAllister, had custody of the crozier, and in 1964 she decided to sell it to the National Museum. John O'Loan and David Kennedy negotiated the sale. The money raised went towards the upkeep of Feystown Church, Glenarm, where a copy of the crozier can be seen at the altar-rails door. The crozier was used for many purposes. At some point the entire shaft had been burnt away, and some of the stones were missing, but now it has been carefully restored.

The Dog's Nose, about three miles north of Garron Point, is so called because of its shape or because of the coldness of the spot. It is a well-loved landmark. A little further north is the White Lady's Grandmother, which is not so well known. It is a gray-shawled figure with a bundle of sticks on her back, bending towards the mountain.

The fields and farms were bright with snow, and the moon was on its wane. The coach that ran to Cushendall was out on the road again. The ghostly wheels went rumbling round, but they left no mark or stain. The coach that ran to Cushendall travelled through the deep snow, the driver cracked the whip and white-faced passengers sat in the coach wrapped in shawls. They leaned across the rattling doors to watch the snow; for them the road to Cushendall was long. Along by Drumnasole, along by Fallowvee on one hand looms the hills, and on the other the lonely sea. The ghostly coach-horn wakes again the echoes that used to be. He who hears the echoing horn will stare as the ghost coach goes by on the road that it used to travel, with rattling wheels that leave no mark in the snow.

Lurigethan, a large flat-topped mountain, spreads towards Cushendall. Lurigethan was one of the first mountains I could recognize and name. On one side is deep Glenariff, the third glen, and perhaps the most beautiful.

The low-back car might be called a convertible. It was simply a low-back car with a roller instead of wheels. It was often used for carting wrack into the fields, and its low body meant it could also be used to carry large stones. Where corn or barley was planted, the land was first harrowed using a wooden harrow with iron tines. The fields were then rolled to produce a firm tilth in which the seeds would germinate quickly.

On large farms in the Glens it was usual to use iron rollers made at Kane's Foundries in Larne or Ballymena, or in Kennedy's in Coleraine, but in the small mountain farms in the Glens wooden rollers were quite common. They were probably made in a joint effort by the local carpenters and blacksmiths.

The coast road is of great geological interest, for extensive landslips have been caused by the water flowing over the soft marls of the lias. An old black-and-white photograph shows how the chalk has slipped on the lias at Garron Point, leaving the basaltic layer on the same level as the chalk beside it. When William Bald built the coast road in the 1830s he realized that the slippery nature of the lias would cause the chalk and basalt to spread over the newly made road. He solved the problem by building horizontal arches, or, as he described it, by adopting the arch principle on a lateral plane.

I look out from Ballygally to the Long Blue Head at Garron Point – one of the most outstanding headlands of the Antrim coast. It is not as rugged as Fair Head, but it creates a lovely backcloth to Red Bay. Garron comes from the Gaelic *gearr rinn*, meaning 'a short headland'. Moira O'Neill, poetess of the Glens, has referred to it in one of her poems as the long blue head of Garron from the sea. In the photograph below the sea is calm, and a man can be seen sitting on the rocks and looking out into the bay. This may be the photographer, W. A. Green. There is not a cloud in the sky.

Long Blue Head, Garron Bay.

Another photograph shows the feeding of the pigs, usually kept in a sty and allowed to roll around the yard. Potatoes were used to supplement the diet of pigs – generally small boiled potatoes, known as chats, or *poreens* or *spachan*. The pig feed was emptied into a wooden trough so that two or three pigs, or a sow and her litter,

49

could be fed at the same time. The photograph shows a cottage with a half-door that let in light and kept out any farm animals that were roaming about. The cottage is painted white and has a thatched roof. A man stands in the doorway, while his wife feeds the pigs. There is also an outhouse in the background.

Waterfoot was another popular port of call for my parents and me, my father taking still photographs and me pressing down the button on the Bell & Howell cine camera. As yet we did not have the Bolex.

North Antrim is predominantly Catholic. The people of the Glens cherish their faith, and during the Troubles they were, thankfully, free from any kind of bigotry. My father was not an Orangeman, but my Uncle Jim would always on 12 July put out a Union Jack on the front of the garage. As a child I would see the Orangemen parading through Ballygally to where a bus picked them up to take them to Belfast; but, for some reason, I have not got the Orangemen on my 8-mm films. Neither my mother or my father held strong Unionist beliefs, and when my father retired he gave way to a Catholic in Antrim Health Committee as the County Dental Officer.

Both my parents had spent some time in England, living in a variety of places, and it seemed at one time as if they would never return to Ballygally and the Glens, where my Uncle Jim was then living. At length my father got a job in Huntingdonshire, at St Neots, where I was born in a thunderstorm at three o'clock in the morning. I could not make up my mind, as I grew older, whether I was an Englishman or an Irishman.

My parents soon returned to Northern Ireland, but my mother perhaps would have preferred it if they had remained in England. My father opened up a dental practice in Larne, but at length he got the job of assistant County Dental Officer, and eventually he was promoted to the top job. He was in his forties when he went into managerial administration.

He had a lot of hobbies. Before the Second World War he was a radio ham, broadcasting all over the world, and he treasured the radio cards from those he contacted, but during the war he discontinued this hobby for reasons of security.

After the war, he settled in Belfast, in Riverdale Park, but he left there and came to Ballygally in the summer of 1955. I was sad at leaving the Finaghy area, for I had made friends with Hugh Bates and Patricia Tuck, as well as other children at Finaghy Primary School. Before returning to Ballygally my mother would regularly take me by train from Belfast to Larne, and out along the coast road to the bungalow, which was named Glyn-Ouley (Uncle Jim was born in Glyn and his wife was born in Ouley, County Down).

My uncle bought the bungalow at Ballygally for £500 well before the Second World War; he had a business at the docks in Belfast supplying goods to ships, but he left this when he was forty to retire to Ballygally.

I have no photographs of Uncle Jim, but there is plenty of 8-mm film of my parents and my brother, Derek.

In 1962 I wrote an unpublished children's novel called *O'Halloran*, about the Vikings in Ulster; it ran to about 30,000 words, but even though I could not get it published I did not forsake my interest in writing. When I was about eighteen I wrote a letter to the editor of the *Church Times* about the life of St Augustine of Hippo and it was published.

Chapter 3

Glenariff

Red Bay and Waterfoot are at the end of Glenariff, about twenty miles (12.5 km) north of Larne and Ballygally. Red Bay has a fine curved beach at the foot of Glenariff, the largest and most popular of the Glens. The sand on the beach has a red colour, derived from red sandstone, and it also has pretty seashells.

The old black-and-white photograph of Waterfoot reproduced opposite shows its row of houses, known locally as the Terrace. They originally housed miners working in the iron-ore mines. The church of St Killian, opened on 15 September 1839, is on the right of the picture.

It is said that there were difficulties in the erection of this church, and this was attributed to a legend recorded in the Ordnance Survey Memoirs for the parish of Ardclinis. The legend said that a church would not stand at Ardclinis.

The photograph also shows the headland sweeping down to the sea, but the church dominates the scene.

About a century ago, ore mined in Upper Glenariff was brought down to the sea by a narrow-gauge railway along the east flank of the valley. It crossed the road by the White Arch (now unspanned) and ran out to the loading pier, whose foundation piles can still be seen. The ore was destined for Scotland or Cumberland. It is now possible to walk along the line of the old railway track, from the White Arch, up the south-east side of Glenariff.

Waterfoot.

At Red Bay there is an old bridge over the Glenariff River, and there is a caravan site with room for camping.

At Waterfoot, each July, the Glens of Antrim Feis is held. This is Northern Ireland's main venue for Irish dancing, music and games. Waterfoot is sometimes called Glenariff.

Between the village and pier there are several sandstone caves. Nanny's Cave extends about twenty feet into the rock, and it was the home for many years in the nineteenth century of Ann Murray, who lived to be 100 years old. She spun and knitted and sold poteen for a living (poteen being a traditional Glens drink). She got into trouble with the excisemen. A blacksmith installed himself in another cave. The cave just at the entrance to the arch, below the ruin of Red Bay Castle housed a school in the eighteenth century. Its pupils included Dr James MacDonnell, co-founder of Belfast Medical School. This cave is said to have been an escape route from the castle. The caves are situated on a raised beach, and they were formed by the sea when sea level was higher.

The construction of Waterfoot Pier is interesting, for many kinds of rocks from the Antrim coast were used.

At one time the only kind of lighting in the country was the cruise lamp. This was a boat-shaped iron vessel filled with fish oil, with a wick made out of the inside of a rush. Peeling pith was a child's occupation, sitting round the fire in the late evening. A thin strip of the outside of the rush was always left on to prevent the pith from breaking. During the making of the cruises a thin plate of iron was hammered into a mould made out of stone. These dies were last used at Red Bay in about 1798.

Glenariff is scattered with white farmhouses. It is the largest of the Glens. There are many attractions for tourists. The glen has lovely waterfalls, Ess-na-Larach being one of the loveliest. Ess-na-Larach means 'the mare's fall', and Ess-na-Crub means 'the fall of the hoof'. Along the flat bottom of the glen the Glenariff River winds its way to the sea.

The road from the Glens to Ballymena is in some ways even more breathtaking than the coast road.

On Lurigethan there is a cave called Lig-na-Fenia. It is surrounded by a ditch, and giants are said to have once lived there. Finn MacCool was the leader of the giants. Ossian, whose grave is in Glenaan, was his warrior-poet son. There is an ancient Danish fort on the top of Dun Clana-Mourna on the top of Lurigethan.

Glenariff Forest Park, where there is an exhibition centre, was called 'a Switzerland in miniature' by the famous author Thackeray. The mountains rise high on each side, with a green and fertile valley between. Five miles (3 km) inland the valley narrows to a deep, wooded gorge with waterfalls thirty-three feet (10 metres) and more in height. Rainbows form in the rising spray.

In the spring and early summer the upper glen is full of primroses and many other attractive ferns and flowers, including wild hyacinths. Trees arch overhead.

Ess-na-Crub, Ess-na-Larach and Tears of the Mountain are the main cascades in ascending order. A path winds round the sides of the gorge, with dramatic views of the falls.

Henry McNeill of Larne was perhaps the first in the modern age to appreciate the beauty of Glenariff and its tourist potential. The LMS railway company built a railway to the glen along the old mineral-railway line, which ran from Ballymena to Parkmore. The company bought the part of the glen around the falls and built a pathway and bridge across the river to provide spectacular views of the waterfalls. The coming of the railway gave a great tourist boost to the region.

Tears of the Mountain.

Tourists from Belfast travelled on the main line from Ballymena; then they changed over to the narrow-gauge railway, which brought them to Parkmore Station. Here wagonettes awaited them, to bring them to the head of the glen at Glenariff Post Office, only about a mile's walk from the cataracts, rushing streams and rugged paths of the glen. In summer there is semi-darkness beneath the trees, but in some areas the sun shines through the vegetation. The Glen is alive with wildlife, and in springtime the birds provide a lovely chorus to accompany a trip into Glenariff. There are many kinds of trees, and the glen is many thousands of years old. It must have been appreciated by ancient man before the birth of Christ.

There are legends of fairies in the glen. The poets, or bards, of ancient Ireland sang the praises of the glen. Lovers would frequent the glen both before and after sunset, listening to the wind in the trees and the sound of the rushing water. Glenariff is a region of great natural beauty, and I must have made fifteen minutes of film about the glens of Antrim as a whole.

Tourists greet one another as they wend their way amongst the trees. The narrow paths were made many thousands of years ago, for ancient man was perhaps also a bit of a tourist.

A tea house at Glenariff provides a welcome resting place. The design of this wooden chalet-like building originated from Thackeray's comment in 1872 that Glenariff was like Switzerland in miniature.

The return fare from Belfast to Glenariff in 1900, first class, was seven shillings and sixpence; second class was five shillings and ten pence; and third class was four shillings.

Tourists to the glen in the nineteenth century and early twentieth century were mainly middle-class, for those fares to the glens were too expensive for the working classes. The tourists from the city were therefore mostly Protestants, as Protestants had a privileged place in Northern Ireland society in those years.

Glenariff, like the other glens, was sparsely peopled, and little farms were in the deep valley.

There is a spectacular view from the head of the glen into Waterfoot and across the North Channel. Photography was just coming into its own in 1900, but tourists still flocked to the glen to paint its beautiful scenes.

Ireland was united with Great Britain, but there were few tourists from the mainland.

Red Bay is noted for its castle, which dominates the skyline. John and Walter Bisset, who had been banished from Scotland in 1242 for the murder of their uncle, bought the Glens of Antrim from Richard de Burgh, and they are said to have been the builders of Red Bay Castle. It was through the marriage of the descendant Margery Bisset to John Mor MacDonnell that the Glens became the property of the Earl of Antrim. The red sandstone cliff is peppered with caves, and it was in one of these that Dr James MacDonnell, founder of the Belfast Medical School, received his early education from a schoolmaster called Michael Traynor.

Desolation is one of the characteristics of parts of the Antrim Glens and its coast, and Red Bay can seem very desolate on a stormy winter's day, overlooked by the ruin of the castle on the headland.

Red Bay, like the other places along the coast, has strong connections with Scotland. Red Bay has an impressive pier. It is one of the most sheltered harbours on the Antrim coast. Here the Vikings must have pulled their ships up on the shore in the eighth and ninth centuries. The Vikings had long had their eyes upon Ulster, for they had heard of the rich monasteries of the land, and they pestered Ireland for some centuries before their final defeat in the eleventh century when the High King of Ireland defeated them in a great battle near Dublin. The Vikings plundered the Glens, carrying treasure back to Scandinavia in their long ships. Coming from the north, the Vikings landed first at Rathlin Island around AD 795. Their base was in York, in the north of England, and from here they would march across the land to take ships from the west coast to Ireland.

The castle at Red Bay was also used extensively by the Bissets and MacDonnells in their comings and goings across the narrow sea to visit their parent clan in Scotland. More recently it was the terminus for a ferry to Campbeltown. I often thought of travelling from Red Bay to Scotland with my motorbike, but alas! it never happened. I had to put up with the trip from Larne to Stranraer on my way to Manchester, where I lived for fourteen years and where I wrote six of my books on Irish history.

Red Bay.

At Parkmore Forest there is a Department of Agriculture caravan site. Close by is the old railway station of a former narrow-gauge railway from Ballymena, and a search may reveal part of the old Black Causeway – a medieval road of flat slabs that led from the Bann Valley to the Glens and the Antrim coast.

The cliffs of Lurig tower above the road like an alpine valley, and small waterfalls can be seen.

On the headland, there is a remarkable promontory fort protected by a multiple defensive earthwork on the landward side.

Some of the stories about Finn MacCool, the Ulster warrior, and his son Ossian, the poet, seem to be set in this region. Hundreds of poems are ascribed to Ossian, or Oisin, but little is recorded about him.

On both sides of the glen small fields ascend like ladders. Some are a relic of the eighteenth-century rundale system of scattered holdings. Today the valley is well drained, and potatoes, dairy products and cattle are sent to Ballymena and Belfast.

The Moyle Way runs from Glenariff to Ballycastle via Trostan, Orra More and Knocklayd mountains and the forests of Slieveanorra and Breen. The Moyle Way starts at pretty Essathothan Glen, in Parkmore Forest.

Tiveragh is a little rounded hill – or fairy hill, as it is known to the locals. It is a volcanic plug, according to some geographers, and it overlooks Red Bay. It is a homely spot, but it can also have an atmosphere of the supernatural. Tiveragh means 'hill of the fort'.

Francis Turnly brought the village of Cushendall in 1801, but he continued to reside at Drumnasole, near Carnlough. The coast road had not yet been built, and he found the daily journey to Cushendall hazardous, for he had to travel over each of the headlines. At length he blasted his way through a protruding crag at Garron Point, and this became known as Turnly's Cut. He also tunnelled through the headland near Waterfoot in 1817, creating an arch thirty-six feet long, twenty-two feet wide and thirty feet high.

In the caves in the Red Bay area there was a blacksmith's forge, and at other times the caves were used by smugglers for their stores. In 1849 workmen found two bronze axes, a stone axe and some silver coins in what was once a cave.

The MacDonnells, in their efforts to dominate the Glens and coast, resided for a while at Red Bay Castle, but Red Bay Castle is not so well known as Dunluce Castle on the Causeway Coast, which also boasts the Giant's Causeway.

Ships carrying warriors from Scotland anchored in the region to assist the Antrim MacDonnells in their fighting efforts. The MacDonnell clan rose to dominate the entire north-east coast of County Antrim, and were a thorn in Queen Elizabeth's side in the sixteenth century. The Glens are isolated from the rest of Ulster by the Antrim Hills, so the English never really penetrated the region until the eighteenth century. That was the start of British ascendancy throughout Ireland, and Dublin Castle became the centre of government.

Chapter 4

Glenballyeamon

This glen sweeps down to the sea towards the little town of Cushendall, at the very heart of the Glens. One can see the outline of ancient forts, but it is a fairly bare glen. A lot of sheep graze on the slopes. At the top of the glen is the terminus of a narrow-gauge railway, and the ruins of a castle. There is supposed to be a fairy tunnel here, where fairy music was said to have lured the unwary. One had to beware!

A raised beach at Cushendall provides a level grassy area on which were held two important events in the calendar of the Glens folk – Cushendall Annual Regatta and Sports (held on 15 August) and the Glens of Antrim Feis (held on the first Sunday in July). The grassy area, convenient to the sea, was known as Legg Green, and it was paramount in bringing the regatta and sports parts of the events together. The first Glens of Antrim Feis was hosted by Glenariff in 1904.

Tievebulliagh is a pointed hill overlooking the glen, beloved by artists and painters, and it is famous for its ancient flint factory. From here flints were exported to other parts of the British Isles and even as far afield as Europe. Nearby, the rounded cone of Trostan, at 1,817 feet, is the highest mountain in County Antrim.

Glenballyeamon is celebrated in 'The Balleamon Cradle Song':

> Rest tired eyes for a while,
> Sweet was its baby smile.

Angels were guarding and watching over you . . .
The birdeens sing a fluting song
And they sang for him all day long.
Wee fairies would dance in the dell for the love of him.
The primrose in the sheltered nook,
The crystal stream, the babbling brook.
Twilight and shadows fall . . .

Cushendall has been called a cosy town, and it has earned the title of the Heart of the Glens, or simply the Town. Here you could learn all the gossip and goings-on of the Glens. There were builders, dairies, garages, shops, etc. Charabancs (big open carts with folded-down roofs) took tourists from Cushendall on conducted tours in times past. After a visit to the Ould Lammas Fair at Ballycastle it wasn't unusual for some of the passengers to have had too much to drink.

Cushendall Bay.

In the centre of Cushendall, at the crossroads beside the square Curfew Tower, a bridge spans the shallow, brown River Dall. Here the boys liked to meet for a crack. At one time the tower was a gaol, and a curfew bell rang from it each night. Behind the tower is a steep hill descending to the old or middle road to Cushendun; and there is a fair green, where fairs were held not so long ago. On a very steep hill descending to the main street is Martin's Court. It was a marvellous place for rolling Easter eggs. The little schoolhouse there welcomes the visitor every Christmas, cosy with oil lamps.

Dusty Rhodes, whose real name was James Stoddart Moore, was born at the old corn mill that used to stand on the Ballycastle road about a quarter of a mile from Cushendall. His father came from Scotland and was a humble shoemaker in Cushendall. James was born on Christmas Day 1844. His mother was a Cushendall woman, Catherine Graham, the daughter of a small farmer. James was the only child of his marriage, and at fourteen years of age he was left as an orphan, his parents having died of fever within six weeks of each other. James was taken into the charge of his aunt, with an inheritance of £100, so that he might receive a good education. However, the sea was calling to him, and he set out to travel the world. He had many careers – miner, soldier, dealer – but the beauties of the Glens never ceased to amaze him, so he started to write poetry. His first wife was Maggie McAllister, who lived in Cushendun. His second wife was Elizabeth Hamill, a Carrickfergus woman. Eventually he found himself living in Coleraine, where he became a tramp, and here his nickname was Dusty Rhodes, after the old grey duster coat he wore. Several of his poems were published by the *Northern Constitution*, and a small collection was made by a friend who did not want the poems to be lost to posterity. Dust Rhodes expressed his love for Cushendall in a poem called 'Bunandalla' (Cushendall). He started off by saying that he had travelled quite a lot – he had seen the haunts of Hindustan and Canton's pagodas. He had seen the Burmese valleys where the leopards stray. He longed for Bunandalla, on Antrim's rocky shore. He often thought of bygone days, when he used to walk there. But now, alas! he found himself bowed down by age, and he cast his longing eye around, looking for peace in vain. He sighed for Cushendall and its pleasant scenes. He used to climb Lurigethan's slopes and Trostan's lofty brow. He gazed on scenes of beauty that he could not gaze at now. He missed the sunny hills, and the mountain gales. On Crock-na-creigh he had often sat on long summer's days. There were woods beneath his feet where the peaceful village lay. He cried out in praise of Cushendall: By the flowery hill of Tiveragh where elfin watchfires glow, there were the wooded slopes of sweet Shramore, where the waters of Dalla flowed. By Alta-a cooin's sylvan shades he could stray. At length he left Bunandalla and the flowery valleys. He often thought of Garron Point and Nappin's fair woodlands, and he sighed for Cushendun and its great scenes of beauty.

The name Cushendall amazes some people. It should be pronounced 'Cus' and it means 'at the foot of the River Dall'.

Near the ruins of the little church at Ardclinis near Red Bay is a stream that flows down the face of the mountain and then passes into a tunnel, where it flows underground until it reaches the sea. I wonder whether this river has some connection with the name Dall (blind). A stranger, Dallas by name, was slain by Ossian in folklore, and some think that the River Dall is named after him. Others believe that the name is connected with the fact that the Dall is a merging of two rivers, the Glenaan River and the Glenballyeamon River. At one time a landlord tried to change the name of Cushendall to Newtownglens, and for a while it appeared so on maps and in the *Parliamentary Gazetteer of Ireland*. However, the people of the Glens did not like the idea, and now the old name is again used. At another time it was also known as Bunandalla, meaning 'the bottom of the River Dall', but this was changed to Cushendall ('the foot of the River Dall').

Lands between Cushendun and Cushendall were in 1687 leased by the 3rd Earl of Antrim to his illegitimate son, Daniel MacDonnell, for a period of 500 years at a rent of £5 per year. After the defeat of James II at the Battle of the Boyne in 1690, Captain MacDonnell departed for Europe with the King and never returned, so his estates were forfeited. In 1702 the estate was bought by the Hollow Sword Blade Company for £2,596. The company made swords with hollow backs into which quicksilver was poured so that there would be an impetus to the blow.

The Glens of Antrim Hotel was one of the important buildings listed in Dobbs' survey of the Glens, carried out in 1817. The construction of the hotel was started by William Richardson and completed by Francis Turnly. By the middle of the nineteenth century seawater bathing had become popular, and a bathhouse was built for hotel guests. Salt water was brought to it from the shore in barrels by horse and cart.

Legg House is believed to have been the house of the Breckenridges, who were well known for their smuggling. They had also a house on Rathlin Island and another near Machrihanish on the Mull of Kintyre, which was also used for their smuggling purposes. In 1938 Legg House became the headquarters of the Cushendall Golf Club, and after many renovations the original house has disappeared. The clubhouse has provided a handy venue for the Glens of Antrim Historical Society for lectures in local history. The society has published a number of books about the history of the Glens, including *An Historical Account of The MacDonnells of Antrim*, a long, well-researched book by George Hill.

At Lurig, from the River Dall, there is a striking view of a mountain at the foot of which is a large pond. For hundreds of years, perhaps, there has existed a pond here. The area between the mountain and the pond became the Cushendall Golf Course in 1938, and so it is preserved for posterity. The hill in the background is called Lurigethan, and there are the remains of an old rath, which is said to have been the living quarters of the warrior-poet Ossian. There is also a large dyke or fortification enclosing about forty acres known as Lignafenia ('the hollow of the warriors').

Like so many villages in the Glens, Cushendall lies in a hollow at the foot of a glen – in this case, Glenballyeamon ('the glen of Edward's town'). On the skyline looms Tiveragh ('the hill of the fairies'). One aged resident of the region, interviewed on the radio about fifty years ago, said that he had witnessed a hurling match between two teams of fairies on the lower slopes of Tiveragh.

Cushendall is impressive on a busy day. The main street is called Bridge Road. The pace of life is such that people still have time for a chat about the rich history of the area. McGrath's Central Bar will sell you some famous old whiskeys; alternatively, you can call in to the chemist shop for a cure! There is ice cream to be had as well as fruit ices.

Elizabeth I intended that the village of Burney Dall, as it was known, should be given to the sons of Henry Knowles, Treasurer of the Royal Household, but it fell into the hands of an adventurer named Surgeon Richardson. It was he who changed the name of the village to Newtownglens. Francis Turnly of Drumnasole bought the village from Surgeon Richardson for £24,000 in 1801, the year in which the Act of Union came into force.

The names on the shop fronts of Cushendall reflect the Scots connection – McAlister, McNeill, McSparran, McKillop, McCollam, McFetridge, McCambridge, and McIlreavy.

There is a good view of the Curfew Tower from Shore Street, and it is at the centre of Cushendall. It was built by Francis Turnly in 1809 as a gaol for riotous persons. Turnly gave instructions that the tower was to be stocked with food to last one year, and he appointed Dan McBride, an army pensioner, to be the permanent garrison of one man – he was not to leave it, day or night. McBride was armed with one musket, a bayonet, a pistol and a pike thirteen feet long with a cross of wood or iron on its handle so that it could be pulled through the hole at the doorway. The lowest projecting windows on each of the tower's four sides had openings for pouring molten substances upon any attackers below.

At one time there was a meeting house at Mullarts, halfway between Cushendall and Cushendun, but the services were moved to Cushendall, where they were held in a school at Court McMartin. The foundation stone of the present church was laid on 15 September 1899 on a site granted by John Turnly. The rent was two shillings per year, and it was opened on 17 June 1900 by the moderator of the General Assembly, the Right Reverend J. M. Hamilton of Donore, County Dublin. The church itself has not got a very exciting exterior, for Presbyterians prefer simplicity to the colour and more elaborate architecture of the Roman Catholic Church.

The Catholic church at Cushendall has a spire, and there is a small cross above the entrance. It lies towards the west of the village on the road to Ballycastle. It was built by Father John McKenna, PP, on a piece of land granted by Francis Turnly. The original church was eighty-four feet long and thirty-two feet wide, and cost the vast sum of £1,000 to build. It was dedicated for worship by the Most Reverend Dr Denvir, Bishop of Down and Connor, on 18 September 1836. It was rebuilt in 1914 and the plans were drawn up by W. J. Moore, a Belfast architect. Even though Catholic emancipation had been granted by Parliament in 1829, the Catholic Church was still a frowned-upon body. Its churches were full of images of Christ and the Virgin Mary, and the Protestants accused the Church of Rome of being heretical. Unlike Protestants, Catholics look to the Pope as their supreme and infallible head, and there is not so much reading of the Bible.

Chapter 5

Glenaan

Only a short distance from Cushendall we come to Glenaan and Ossian's Grave in a place called Lubitavish on the River Dall. A little verse has been written about it. I am dreaming too, when the twilight closes on the house. There were the ash-crowned rath and gentle places where Finn and Ossian loved to stray. There is the thorn bush and the fairy fountain where the midnight moon lingered. There is the cairn high on the misty mountain, and the solemn calm of the countryside.

Glenaan has a swift river bubbling over boulders down the middle of the Glen, and it is a bare and open place.

Ossian's Grave, which can be described as a two-chambered horned cairn, can be found a little way up Glenaan. It is said to be the last resting place of Ossian, the warrior-poet of the third century, son of Finn MacCool. The grave, though, is older than this, dating back to 2000 BC. Ossian was the leader of the Fianna, a bold band of warriors that fought and sang in ancient Ireland. They were a brotherhood, and Ossian was not only a leader but also one of their greatest poets. He had by his side his brave warrior son, Osgar, who perished in the battle between the Fianna and the High King of Ireland and his men. He was deeply missed by both Finn and Ossian. Only twice did Finn shed tears: for Osgar and for his beloved dog, Bran. After this bloody battle and the loss of so many warriors, the remainder of the Fianna were out hunting one day when a beautiful girl came towards them on a white horse. She had long golden locks, blue eyes and cheeks that were redder than a rose. She was called

Niamh of the Golden Hair, and she was the daughter of the King of the Country of the Young. She said that she had heard of the greatest deeds of Ossian and had come to give him her love. Ossian was overpowered by her beauty and the thought of the delightful countryside where she would take him. He said to her that she was his choice beyond all the women in the world and he would go with her willingly. Ossian mounted his horse, followed her to the shore and disappeared towards the sea. When his friends saw this, they cried out three times, and they never saw Ossian again.

After many years in the Country of the Young, Ossian came back to Erin, and he was found, an old man, lying on the ground. By then St Patrick had reached Ireland in the fifth century and Ossian was carried to him. He stayed in the saint's house and had long talks with him. Patrick tried to convert him to Christianity, but Ossian said that he had no liking for clerks, for their music was not sweet. Patrick could not talk him out of grieving, for Finn and all the brave Fianna had now gone.

A poem by Sydney Bell is entitled 'Ossian's Grave, Lubitavish'. They say it was here that Ossian died. And he wondered if bright-haired Niamh cried whose lovely fingers piled the cairn and heaped it high with maiden fern. The peewits cried out, though they never had seen the name of the one that loved Ossian. I hope and hope that he found somewhere his slender Niamh of the Golden Hair, for there was a song too brief to scan with some bones, and an old blind man.

Ossian's Grave is a later Stone Age court grave and stone circle at the top of a lane in the Glen, two and a half miles (4 km) west of Cushendall on the east side of Tievebulliagh.

It is not clear whether Ossian took the strictures of St Patrick seriously; certainly the saint wanted to convert him and perhaps take him on his missionary journeys. Slemish, where Patrick had been enslaved, lies about twenty miles (30 km) inland in County Antrim, and he would have talked to Ossian about his experiences as a slave. Patrick would have admired the poetry of Ossian, and perhaps the poet wrote verse about the Catholic Church. Patrick had headed for Rome after he escaped from Slemish, and eventually Pope Celestine I gave him the task of evangelizing Ireland. There was, perhaps, Christianity in Ireland several hundred years before the arrival of Patrick. Patrick reached Ulster in AD 432, after landing at Downpatrick in County Down, where he established the first church in the island. There is a stone slab marking his burial place. Along with St Columba and St Brigid, he is one of the three great saints of Ireland.

Ossian's Grave, Cushendall.

Without doubt, St Patrick reached the Glens, but it is not clear which of the Glens was his favourite. In *Confession*, St Patrick's spiritual autobiography, he talks of a paradise somewhere in Ireland where he contemplated the life and faith of the Church. Perhaps Glenaan was his favourite spot! He brought with him to Ulster a simple Christian faith, without the sophistications of later centuries, but it is sure that he held the Virgin Mary in great esteem. He prayed to her by day and night. The Bible had taken shape by St Patrick's time, and he searched the Scriptures and explained the doctrine of the Trinity to the Gaels of Glenaan using a three-leafed shamrock.

Little churches, seating a small number of worshippers, sprang up in the Glens. These churches were made of stone or wood.

The Christianity that Patrick brought to the region was mainly monastic, but there are no remains of ancient monasteries in Glenaan or, for that matter, elsewhere in the Glens. Patrick established the Primatial see at Armagh in AD 455, using it as a base to evangelize all the Gaels of Ireland.

Today there are two Archbishops of Armagh: one for the Catholic Church and one for the Church of Ireland, which also claims to be the 'Catholic' Church. Today Glenaan is a mainly Roman Catholic community. However, the two sides, Protestants and Catholics, have a better understanding of their faith as a result of the effects of radio and television in the region.

Chapter 6

Glencorp and Glendun

Glencorp is an inland glen, linking Glenaan and Glendun. The hedges in the glen are a riot of fuchsia and honeysuckle in summer. Between the main Cushendall–Cushendun road and the sea, two older roads over the hills offer a scenic view. At Cushkib, just over a mile west of Layde Church, two mound forts stand side by side and are called twin towers. A twenty-six-mile (41 km) stretch of the Ulster Way passes over the summit of Trostan (1808 feet), Orra More (1667 feet) and Knocklayd. A road runs through this small glen. It is a gentle place of small hills and farms, and there is a line of trees on the skyline above the glen.

There is the song of Glendun, the seventh glen. The fairy thorn is in flower and it fills the heart. Flower of May, flower of May, what about the May time, and he far away? Summer is lovely in the green glen, the white birds love the sea, and the wind must kiss the heather top, and the red bell hides a bee. As the bee is dear to the honey flower, so one is dear to the traveller. Flower of rose, flower of rose. A thorn pricked the traveller one day. The bracken up the braeside has rose scent in the air, and three birches lean together, silver-limbed and fair. Golden leaves are flying fast, but the scarlet type is rare. Berry o' the rowan! Berry o' the rowan! The wind sighs amongst the trees, but the traveller sighs alone. The traveller sits beside the turf fire, and the winter nights are for thinking long.

Moira O'Neill described Glendun as a steep-sided, well-wooded glen with the turf-brown Dun River tumbling over the many rocks

68

and boulders and slowing to a spread upon reaching the valley. She said it was a grand place for fishing when there was a flood on. The hill farms are approached by swaying bridges or by fording the river. Many bridges were destroyed in a recent landslide, but they have been replaced by steel structures. There, in the wee pool of Dunurgan, old Murray spotted the fine salmon when he went to fetch a bucket of water. The salmon was a beauty, the dog lay on the grass then made a dive and caught the salmon between its teeth and landed him. A bang with a stone did the rest. At a spot higher up, some of the poachers tried dynamite – a cruel way to go about the job. Past the whitewashed chapel and Craigagh Wood with its Altar in the Woods, the Dun River runs under the old arched bridge to meet the sea at Cushendun.

The Altar in the Woods is a very ancient stone with a carving of a crucifix and a winged cherub above it. The stone was carried from Scotland to be used as an altar by Catholics during the period of the Penal Laws. The people met for worship beneath an old oak, but they wanted a special stone – a good stone – to mark the meeting place. Some men from the Glens rowed across the North Channel to Scotland and brought the stone back, and it may have been from the island of Iona. There is a fine church nearby, and every year in the month of June many people come to pray at the old altar.

Nearby in the little churchyard of Craigagh Church is another interesting stone. This stone marks the burial place of Charles McAllister, who died at the great age of ninety-seven. Charles McAllister and Nelson were shipmates for twenty-two years. They were together on the *Cucass*, and later they were partners in the Battle of the Baltic, but Nelson was feeling depressed.

Horatio said to Charlie, "I doubt it is all up with us."

Charlie replied, "Hold your tongue; rake your guns and you will be all right."

This advice was taken and the battle was won.

On the tombstone there is a rough drawing of a little ship anchored at both ends, with the inscription: 'Your ship, love, is moored head and stern for a fuldiew'. Some say that the ship is the ship of war in which McAllister sailed with Nelson; others believe it is the lower left quartering of the McAllister arms (the quartering is similar to that of the MacDonnells). There is also on the stone

Cushendun.

A Glendun farm kitchen.

carving something representing McAllister as a 'scapegoat'. The late Sam Henry, folklorist, discovered that when a ship was laid up for any reason the sailors received ample leave; in this case the leave was for eternity. It is said that when Nelson was parting with Charles he offered him three choices: he might have a permit of freedom from curfew restrictions; he might save a man from the gallows; or he might receive fifty guineas.

There is a tale in the Tripartite Life that St Patrick was displeased with St Olcan over a certain matter, and he said that St Olcan's lands would be given to St MacNissi and to Seanan of Innis Altic ('the island of the birds'). O'Laverty equates Innis-Pollan with Innis Altic. Seanan was a bishop in this region of North Antrim, so that saint may have had a direct connection with the church in this area. Seanan's Isle is on the river near Glendun Church.

The following song about an exile's longing for home is from the eighteenth century. It was originally sung in Irish. It is believed that it refers to the townland of Ardicoan, near Glendun. In another translation, this song is called 'The Quiet Land of Erin'. It has been sung by Mary O'Hara.

If I were in Aird a' Chumhaing near the mountain that was far from him, he would be always paying a visit to the Glen of the Cuckoo on Sunday. His heart was heavy and sad. For many Christmases he would be in Cushendun and all alone, playing on the white strand with his hurley stick in his hand. He was not, however, weary of being by himself for he heard the voices of the birds – sparrow, thrush and snipe – and he was not aware that it was Sunday. It would be a great achievement to entice the sheep from the lamb. If he had a skiff with oars, he would take himself on the ridge of the waves, and he swore that he would die in Ireland.

The little village of Cushendun is now in the care of the National Trust. It was described by St John Irvine as the most beautiful village in the world. It is called Bun-abhannDuin in *The Annals of the Four Masters*. It was later changed to Cois-abhann-Duine ('the foot of the River Dun'), which has been altered to the present name. It is the nearest Irish port to Britain. According to the Reverend Dobbs, writing in the early nineteenth century, Cushendun used to be a busy port, having a lot of traffic with the Mull of Kintyre – sending over black cattle and Highland ponies. Cushendun is a Cornish-style village, and is beloved by painters and poets. Here the blue lips of the sea reach for the amber bowl of the land. The small beach at Cushendun is full of pebbles, and one can spend many hours searching for precious stones. There are some beautifully polished stones; also, the farmers drew many a load of stones and sand for their various needs from the Cushendun shore.

The caves at the rear of the hotels are famous and unusual. They are of sandstone conglomerate, and they provide a fearful entrance to the Cave House that lies beyond. In Mr Crommelin's time he had storerooms here, a powder magazine, a smith's forge and a cow-house. The famous poet John Masefield met his bride at Cushendun, and he says:

> In the curlew-calling time of Irish dusk
> Life becomes more splendid than its husk.

Moira O'Neill was known as the Poet of the Glens, and her poems have been famous for over sixty years. She was born in the large square white house by the bay. Her maiden name was Nesta Higginson, and she lived in Canada after her marriage, but eventually she returned to the south of the Ireland. Her poems are still in great demand.

The little rivulet of Brabla' Burn is featured in several of her poems. It bubbles down the hill near Milltown – an assemblage of houses behind Cushendun Bay.

Her poem 'Cuttin' Rushes' starts by saying that it may have been yesterday or fifty years ago that she rose early in the morning for the cutting of the rushes. She would walk up to the Brabla' Burn, but still the sun was low. She would hear the burn run and then she would hear the thrushes. She would cry out to a lad that sported the wet grasses of honeysuckle hanging sweetly down: Here, lad, would he follow where she passes, and find her cutting rushes on the mountain. Was it only yesterday or only fifty years ago that they sat around the dog pools high amongst the heather. The hook had made his hand sore, so she had to leave, and it was for her that he cut the rushes to bind together. Come back! Come back along the burn and see the lovely honeysuckle hanging like a crown. They were after cutting rushes on the mountain.

Another poem is 'Grace for Light'. When they were little children they had a wee square house, away up amongst the heather by the head of Brabla' Burn. They would see the hares as they were shooting, and they would hear the crowing grouse. At night they had hardly any room in the little house. She would put the youngest two to bed, their faces to the wall. However, they could sit around as they wished. A torch was lit within for them all, and God should be thanked, she would say, now that they had light. They thanked God that their sins should be forgiven. He put his pipe down, and said some inspiring words: May the Lamb of God lead them to salvation. The nine Glens of Antrim provide spectacular sights, but not their poor little house where they lived at Brabla' Way, nor a child in all the Glens that had seen the light.

On the side of the bay was a little cottage whose owner was known as John o' the Rocks. He was a McNeill, and his cottage was a favourite subject for painters. Now there is a modern house on the site.

On the steep road that runs to Torr Head is a cairn erected to the memory of Shane O'Neill, or Shane the Proud as he became known. Shane was murdered at Carra Castle, near Cushendun, in 1567 by the Antrim MacDonnells, with whom he had taken refuge. After supper a fight broke out and Shane died as the result of many wounds. According to Dr D. A. Chart in *A History of Northern Ireland*, his body was wrapped in a soldier's old shirt and flung into a pit. His head was cut off and taken to Dublin in order that the reward might be claimed from the government there. It was an ignominious end for such a fine warrior.

The graveyard here is known as Cross Sbreen. There is also a monument here to Roger Casement.

Between Torr Head and Cushendun the road is known as the Road of Lady Londonderry. One day she set out for a drive in her coach with her new English coachman at the reins. Past the village the road became more and more dangerous, so Lady Londonderry decided to turn back, but this was impossible because of the narrowness of the track. It was so narrow that two carts could not pass. At last the horses were taken out of their harnesses and an army of labourers was summoned; gradually they manhandled the coach round, and Lady Londonderry was able to return, thankfully, to Cushendun.

Another challenging road here is known as the Corkscrew Road.

It climbs from Cushendun in a series of zigzags to join the road from Ballycastle to Cushendall.

Torr Road, too, with its striking views of cliffs and delightful bays, is twisty and steep. It requires a careful driver.

Torr Head is magnificent. It is the nearest point to Scotland in Antrim. Here great fires were lit by the Antrim Scots when they needed help from their kinsmen in Scotland.

Around Torr are a number of interesting remains. On Torr West, a short distance from the road between Ballycastle and Torr, standing stones are scattered. These are called the Meurogs. The 'finger stones' are supposed to have been flung from Torr Head by a giant.

A short distance west of the Meurogs lies St Columba's Stone, a rude stone three feet long and one foot thick. On its flat side there are some indentations which are said to be impressions of the hand and foot of the saint.

On the massive headland at Torr was a fort called the Fort of the Barach. Barach was the giant who was said to have flung the finger stones at the five other giants near Ballyucan with whom he was having a fight. The headland sweeps down to the sea. The fisherman's anthem once again rang round the headlands wild and clear. The cheery ring of the old refrain was often echoed round by Torr as often as it ran over cliff and hollow, as often as it is sounded round that shore. O, for the short summer nights, when the leaves are green on the woods of Clona! O, for a seaworthy boat, the sails well set, and the wind to follow, the dark-green breakers foaming! They would never again see the sunset on old Kintyre, tingeing the rugged cliffs with gold until all the headlands seem to be on fire. The poet was on Ailsa Craig no more.

The poet in question was Dusty Rhodes.

Murlough Bay is a beautiful, deep-set crescent where gentle woods sweep down to the sea. Until recently it was not accessible to the motorist. It has been opened by the National Trust so that tourists and locals can enjoy the beauty. Here Roger Casement asked to be buried, but it was not to be: a plain Celtic cross (now broken) overlooks the sea in his memory.

St Mologe is associated with Murlough, and in ancient days his grave was well known; today he and his origins are rather hard to trace. A special Mass, called the Fair of Murlough, was held there. It is thought that *Mo* and *Oge* were added to the name of Luan – a saint who originated near Bangor and founded a number of monasteries. On Rathlin Island a monastery called Kilvoruan is associated with him.

There are many other roads from Cushendall. My father's old Ford Prefect followed two delightful winding roads to explore the land between Cushendall and Cushendun. The middle road (a continuation of the steep road up behind the Curfew Tower) passes the old Fair Green, scene of some of the Cushendall Fairs. The road skirts Tiveragh (the fairy hill). An eyewitness described his eerie experiences here, and they will be recalled later in this book. A poem called 'In Tiv-ra Hill near Cushendall' describes what followed when a noise was heard behind a wall:

He stopped and looked over, and exclaimed, "What is making the noise?" It was a hurley match and two small teams of the fairy-folk were ripplin', tearin' and weltun' away. In the moonlight it was as bright as day. Their playing pitch was hardly as big as his Uncle Barney's potato rig. He stood there watching them pluck and clout at the back of the wall with his eyes tightly closed. A wee voice was heard: "Who is up there?" And a bit of a thing about nine inches tall came climbing up to the top of the wall. He stood there, with his fingers up at his eyes. In God's plain truth he was speaking his mind. Aye, that's what he said and what he had said was enough. Did he run? Surely not!

There is a very long tale by Dusty Rhodes about the blacksmith called Robert Kennedy who lived near Tiveragh: come hither for a *shanagh*, come hither, *Shawn agrah*, did he remember Kennedy the smith of Tiveragh. Of course he did not forget, the old man replied, for the hero often fought for Erin by my side. A braver heart could not be found in all the rebel ranks where they nightly assembled on Dalla's mossy banks. A hero true and staunch was he that ever took the field, for the gleaming blade shone in his hand. Seldom near the smithy was Robin to be seen, except when *pilkes* were wanted by the boys that adorned the green. He was an outlaw, barred from social pleasures. His bed was on the slopes of Trostan. Hark! A noise disturbed matters, a sound pleasant to the ears. It was the clanking of the sabre and the yeoman's steady tread. What brings them here from Cushendall on this summer's evening? They were but this night to seek the life of Robin Kennedy. The smith took off his apron and flung his hammer down, and, darting from the smithy door, he dashed through the brown heather. He paused for an instant, but he onward quickly made his way to seek out a safe place on Orra's distant crest. Night was quickly closing in, but still the hunted man stepped forward through the valley of Glendun. Close behind him the yeomen ride with their shining sabres. God help you, Robert Kennedy, you are in extreme danger. He led them on by hill and bawn until it was midnight, past many rugged bereen and many a thorny bower, until he gained a deep morass, a dark and treacherous mere. Kennedy said that they would wet their feet, who came to seek him here. At length the weary captain abandoned Orra's dreary mountain, and he reluctantly turned to it, but in vain, through deep Glendun, past Eagles Hill, amongst Esheragh's boulders grey, but the spot where the blacksmith resided was never found. And there he lay from dawn to day glimmering in the eastern sky. On the far horizon a flame shot high, and he knew that they would find his cottage, but Robin did not mind – they had burned the cage, said Kennedy, the bird they could not find. A price was set upon his head, and they searched the countryside thoroughly from Torr Head to Ballyeamon Glen, but Robin was not to be found.

They searched for many a weary day by Tiveragh's green brae, but they never found the rebel smith, brave Robin Kennedy.

This middle road, with its feathery beech trees, winds forward to meet the Cushendun road near Dunurgan. Here the tourist can look upon the farms of Glencorp and the beauty of the mountains and glens. It is the old road, well known to frequenters of the Glens, where children may roam as free as birds.

A road from the Curfew Tower leads to the sea at Cushendall, but just before coming into the bay another road bears left over the hill. It is the road to Layde, which rises high above Red Bay and the surrounding hills.

The famous burial place of the MacDonnells of Antrim is a great attraction. A secluded mossy lane leads to the hallowed place in a little glen set high above the sea. There is a mysterious silence here and it is unbelievably cool, even on a hot summer's day. Here are numerous gravestones dominated by the fine Celtic cross to the memory of Dr James MacDonnell, a descendant of the famous MacDonnells of the Glens. The cross is decorated with biblical scenes connected with healing, and these are surrounded by Celtic spirals. The inscription describes a man well beloved: 'He was a man whose ability was ever outweighed by his piety.' He was a patron of the old Gaelic harpers, and he kept an open house for some of them. He was also one of the first medics to use chloroform to anaesthetize his patients during operations.

This old graveyard was the burial ground of the senior branch of the MacDonnells – the descendants of Colla of Kilbane Castle, elder brother of Sorley Boy. A direct descendant of Sorley Boy told Maureen Donnelly, author of *The Nine Glens,* about a curious whinstone rock in the old churchyard. She said it has on it a device of the patron saint of the clan. Could this be St Kieran? The coat of arms on several of the gravestones is that of the MacDonnells – featuring the salmon, the deer, the lymphad and the hand grasping the crosslet.

Layde was once the site of a Franciscan monastery. The church was in regular use until 1790. Then services were transferred to a house called The Old Inn in Cushendall, and, at a later date, to Layde Parish Church. An old manuscript states: 'In a dell near the shore, about one mile from Cushendall are the ruins of a small religious house, said to have been founded by the Clan McFall or McFaul.' St Kieran of Clonmacnoise was the patron saint of the church. A well near the road above Layde Church is called St Kiernan's Well. The surname McIlheron means a descendant of the disciple or servant of Kiernan.

In the seventh century this Irish saint travelled to Scotland and lived in a cave near Campbeltown, the old local name being Ceann-loch-cill Ciaran, so called because the saint's original church was built at the head of Campbeltown Bay. In the episcopal Church of Scotland, the present church is dedicated to St Kieran.

From 1696 to 1793 three generations of the same family served at Layde Parish Church. They resided at Tromra. At this time Irish was the language of the Glens, and these three clergymen preached the Protestant religion to the people in their own language. From Castlegreen the road bears west over the mountain, or up the Line, as the Ballycastle road was once called. This road spans Glendun and its river by means of a great viaduct which stands out amongst the many attractions of the Glens. On all sides there is boggy moorland, with bright green patches of grass and waving bog-cotton. It is delightful to the eye and an invitation to roam. There is no monotonous flatness to the moor. Giant grey boulders left by a glacier in the Ice Age lie grouped together. Turf stacks break the skyline – a tribute to the industry of the men of the Glens of Antrim. Sheep graze everywhere – even on the roadside if it suits them. Curlews and seagulls call and swirl. The air is sharp in winter and balmy in summer, and this has its effect on the brittle turf.

A pleasant little poem called 'My Sorrow It Is' by Sydney Bell is set in the Glens of Antrim. It starts by saying that it was his sorrow that the tongue of the Glens had fled. There was to be no smooring of fires this night, and no telling of tales, and no song! There was not a song along the length of the Glens. Where once there was laughter and fun, where once there was dancing, there was now only the dancing leor, and there was only the sun to light the deserted floor. The galbes stand by the fuchsias running wild in all the length of the glen. With the liquid tongue of their sires to keep him company in the long night the women would murmur the Grace for Light.

The Vanishing Lake, or Loughareema, or the Fairy Lough, is crossed by the Ballycastle road. I can now remember my father having a black-and-white photograph of it. One day the water could be almost flooding the road, as it was in the photograph, and on the next day it could be empty, the water having drained away through the underlying chalk. But where did the fish go? My father said that they drained away too. This was the only possible explanation. Moira O'Neill loved the lough, and she made it famous in her poetry. Loughareema! Loughareema! Lies so high amongst the mountain heather, and there was the little lough, a dark lough where herons went fishing and seagulls travelled in from the coast.

However, there was danger here as well as beauty. A man called McNeill perished when his carriage plunged into the waters.

After passing the lake, Ballypatrick Forest looms up, the moorland is shut out and the traveller begins to descend. Soon the Carey River comes in sight, and a landmark called the King's Chair. This region could have once belonged to a wealthy chieftain, for all around there are souterrains, dolmens and duns.

At the end of the mountain road is the tiny village of Ballyvoy and here a shoreward road leads to Torr. Joseph Campbell, another poet, described this road in 'The Golden Hills of Ballyucan': Down from the moorlands a hundred silver streamlets drained before the dawning fire, and the mottled thrushes in the trees sang songs of deep desire to the golden hills of Baile-eocain O.

Loughareema, the Vanishing Lake, Ballycastle.

At Culfreightrin St Patrick is said to have founded a chapel and left a close friend in charge. The great mound of Knocklayd soars up between here and Ballycastle, with our last two glens, Glenshesk and Glentaisie, on either side of the mountain.

A road signposted to Corrymeela leads to a community centre for the reconciliation of the people of Ulster. Corrymeela means 'hill of harmony'. Moira O'Neill's Corrymeela was a little further round the coast towards Cushendun: she wrote that over here in England she was helping with the hay, and wished that she was in Ireland to live long days. She became weary of the English hay, and she thought of Corrymeela and the blue sky over it. There was a deep river flowing beyond the heavy trees, and the air was filled with the noise of humming bees. She wished that she heard the Cladagh burn go running through the heat, past that Corrymeela with the blue sky over it.

Knocklayd is said to have been called after Fergus McLeide, an ancient warrior, but there is another story about a Scots girl, Lydia, who eloped with a young man and landed on a rock in the townland of Layd. Later she fled to Knocklayd, giving her name to both places. He said that people raved about the scenery of the place out in the west, and they say that it was one of the fairest and best, but they do not know the talent that Dame Nature displayed when she touched her canvas and painted Knocklayd.

Knocklayd was once known as Dunlayd, and the name also referred to an extensive part of County Antrim. Perhaps it was one of the names for Dalriada before Cairbre Riada conquered these regions.

On the summit of Knocklayd are the remains of a cairn. One legend has it that three Norwegians were buried there, while another says that it marks the grave of a Scots lady called McLeod and her two children.

It is most likely that Fergus McLeide was the one who gave his name to the mountain.

Chapter 7

Glenshesk

At last we come to the famous Glenshesk! From Ballycastle there is a road leading inland to the V-shaped, well-wooded glen. Glenshesk is wild and unspoilt, and there is a splendid view of Rathlin Island and the Mull of Kintyre.

One of the fascinating things to see in the townland of Carnsampson is Doonfin, a little rath where Finn MacCool's dog died. It is said that Finn tried to console himself by composing lamentations. In an account from Mason's Parochial Survey in 1816 an Irish poem is described, the manuscript being owned by one Charles McIldowney. An ancient chant of six notes, the first four solemn and the concluding two loud and rapid, has been handed down to us by the people of Romoan.

In the woods on the slopes of Knocklayd are the ruins of an old church known as Goban Saer's Castle. There is also a round tower in the grounds at Armoy, at one end of Glenshesk.

Again we call upon the poetry of Dusty Rhodes: As Finn MacCool went hunting one summer's afternoon in dark Glenshesk's deep valley, beneath the silver'd moon, his dog Bran went first, fast on the red deer; he was the bravest dog that ever ran, a dog of ancient fame. He quickly overcame the flying deer, and pulled the quarry down, and slew another of the herd to add to his fame. They returned to his master and soon appeared in view, and his jaws were wide open from which foam ran. Finn MacCool was afraid when he saw the animal running to his master's side, blood dripping from his jaws. He placed an arrow in his bow and drew the string, and with a good fast arrow he slew the faithful greyhound, though when the dog appeared in view, he did not know his fate. From that day onwards Finn became a sad and altered man, still crying out, "I have slain my faithful servant, Bran."

The Buachalan Bwee were soldiers, each in his saffron line, waiting silently. As the traveller walked by the salmon stream in the sea-sounding valley of the glen one day when it was drizzling, with the blue Antrim Hills surrounding him, this was when he met the soldiers.

The poet Florence Wilson has written about the valley: All along the valley the golden soldiers stand, but there was no sound of marching through MacEsmund's land. There was no flashing of the claymore from the glen to the sea. In their huts of green and amber they silently kept watch. They guard the peace of Enan, round Drumsenie's place of prayer, but not for him or Colum do they toss their yellow hair. If they made no pact with Patrick, they kissed him, brow and chin, for down the flock-filled valley his feet came wandering.

Once upon a time in the days of Lammas he heard him wake again, Sorley Boy MacDonnell who called through the rain. The purple heather sighed from Trostan to Knocklayd, each in his tent of hill-mist stirred at the caoine he made. The long sun shadows creep on Eachra's jewelled rim, by Mairge and by Carey they turned and followed him.

All along the valley they lifted their gilded shields, in countryside and townland, and they were lords of the pasture fields. Alas, if only he had followed when his cry rose up the glen, calling out to Sorley Boy MacDonnell and his golden soldier-men!

Chapter 8

Glentaisie

Glentaisie, or Glentow, lies on the western side of Knocklayd. It is a small glen, and the main road from Ballycastle to Armoy runs through it. It is not as desolate as the other glens. The name Taisie is associated with a princess of Rathlin, and there she fled after a great battle.

Again we call upon the poet Dusty Rhodes: Near a high thorn hedge by the side of the way lived a woman of eighty years of age. A few of the people now remember her, and everyone had heard about the old witch of Glentow. She came to the glen, and lay by the side of the river. A bonnet adorned her brow, and everyone feared the old witch of Glentow. A woman refused to give her a meal, and quickly the woman experienced her vengeance. Two sheep had disappeared from the farm and all said that they were killed by the witch of Glentow. Two young fellows swore that they would slay the witch, so one night they carried her off to the seashore and flung her into the breakers. In such a way they drowned the witch of Glentow. After a year the young men died, but the cause of death is not certain. From the river's deep shadow he vowed that the people would often hear the old witch of Glentow.

Another poet, one Joseph Campbell, praised the Glentaisie of the fairy songs: Glenshesk of the brown burns; Glendun that stirs from her sleep while one passes; Glenariff of the leaping waterfalls and silver trees; Glencorp whose name forbids us calling them; Glenballyeamon that was like a battler's queen; Glengorm of the blue glen; Glencloy, the glen of the shadows; and Glenaan, the glen of the little ford.

Bun-na-Margie is the name given to an old Franciscan monastery near Ballycastle. The name means 'the fort of the Margy'. The Margy River is formed by the joining of the Shesk and Carey rivers. The monastery is said to have been founded by Rory McQuillan, Lord of the Route (North Antrim), about the year 1500. Another tale says that it was erected as an act of atonement by Phelim McCormack, who had committed murder.

It is thought that the first battle between the McQuillans and the MacDonnells took place on land adjacent to the monastery. Colla MacDonnell is perhaps buried at Bun-na-Margie along with other MacDonnells. Layde is another of the MacDonnell resting places. Four Earls of Antrim, along with their wives, are buried at Bun-na-Margie.

The ruins are worth visiting. As a child I used to imagine the monks chanting and the priests celebrating Mass.

The monastery, of course, was entirely Catholic, but it suffered under the sacking of the monasteries in the sixteenth century. The church measures ninety-nine feet by 241 feet and there are many interesting carvings to be seen. At the west end is a small cross believed to mark the burial place of Julia McQuillan, the Black Nun of Bun-na-Margie.

The Black Nun was, it appears, a great prophetess, and she was much honoured in her lifetime. One of her prophecies was that Knocklayd would bring forth a great torrent of water which would inundate the land for seven miles around. At her death she was interred at the door of the church, as had been her wish, so that she might be trodden under the feet of those entering.

Dunaneanie Castle ('the fort of the fairs') was built by Alexander MacIan Cathanac MacDonnell, who had fled to the Glens about 1500 from a troubled Scotland. He was Lord of Islay, Kintyre and the Glens, being a direct descendant of John, Lord of the Isles, who in 1399 married Margery, the Bisset heiress of the Glens.

Kinbane Castle ('the castle of the white head') is said to have been built by Alexander's third son, Colla. It is more likely that it was built by his wife, Eveleen McQuillan, when the troubles with the McQuillans were beginning.

Dunamallaght ('the fort of the curse') has an unusual story attached to it. It appears that Donnell Lalacht was the sixth son of Alexander,

Lord of the Isles. His mother, when carrying his child, cursed it as her husband had killed her five brothers in battle, all in a day. She prayed that if she had a daughter, she would be a harlot; or, if it was a boy, that he would never see the light of day. It is said that her prayer was answered. Dunamallaght lies behind Sheskburn House, in Ballycastle.

Fair Head is a great headland at the western end of Murlough Bay. It is sometimes called Benmore.

In a castle on Rathlin Island lived a pretty girl, and she had many suitors, but two of them were so keen for her hand that they fought. It was agreed that the winner should marry the girl. One of them was mortally wounded, and with his dying breath he whispered to his servant to dance with the girl out on the cliffs below the castle. The servant obeyed his master, and they started to dance. They danced nearer and nearer to the edge of the cliff, until the girl fell over. The servant had killed her to avenge his master. The spot where her body was washed up was from then on known as Fair Head, because of the beautiful yellow hair of the drowned girl.

Fair Head and Strand, Ballycastle.

85

On the headland is the Grey Man's Path, supposedly named after a holy man who came to the spot each day for prayer and meditation. However, after his death he took on a more sinister role: he became a ghost, bringing bad luck to all who saw him.

Again we call upon Dusty Rhodes: There was many a rugged rock and bay from Torr to Ballintoy. But from the keep of Dunluce Castle to wooded Cushendall the pathway of the great sea cairn is wildest of them all. A pillared chasm, rude and stern, made by the hand of God from whose high arch of stone the sea sweeps before. It was there, at midnight, that the mystic Grey Man glided along the top of the rugged rocks, down their sloping sides. So there he flew all night long until daybreak. Above the tide, far and wide, rings forth his mystic cry. A good ship headed for the ocean away from Benmore Head and came not near the rocky shore until the fatal hour. His awful form was not for mortal eyes, nor his voice fit for mortal ears to hear.

The name of the townland, Ballyucan, near Fair Head, is said to derive from Bally-jotun, the home of the Nordic giants. On the side of the head is a stone known as Finn MacCool's Finger Stone, which Finn is said to have thrown from the island to chase away a cow that was grazing too near the edge.

The Grey Man has also been associated with the Fir-Li, the storm god of the Danann race of about 1500 BC. The Fir-Li was also believed in by races of the Middle East. Evidence of belief in the Fir-Li can be seen around the coast in Portnoffer, at the Giant's Causeway, and at Rathlin.

A path used by dulse gatherers on the Murlough side of Fair Head is also called Kishla. Mary McAnulty was an old woman who made her living gathering dulse below Fair Head, and the entrance to the Grey Man's Path came to be known as Mary McAnulty's Hall Door. One evening, when she was coming home with a load of dulse, she met a fine gentleman near her 'hall door'. He walked with her to a place not far from Lough Dhu, where she sat down to rest. The stranger asked her to look at his hair and tell her what she saw.

She exclaimed, "It is green!"

"And no wonder!" he said, "for I have lived for many years under the Black Lough."

Murlough Bay and Fair Head, County Antrim.

They walked on for a bit, and again they sat down to rest. This time he put his head on her lap and went to sleep. Mary now noticed his cloven hoofs and she became increasingly alarmed. She slipped away and left him to rest. When he awoke and found his friend gone, the stranger turned himself into a horse and neighed so loudly that he frightened the whole townland. However, Mary had escaped, and it is thought that the extraordinary stranger returned to his home in Lough Dhu.

This, in fact, is the old legend of the *each-uisge*, or water-horse, told in many Celtic lands.

At one time a herd of wild goats lived on the headland.

The Rock of Usnach is a large flat rock lying near the foot of the cliffs here.

A harper to King Conchobar of Emain Macha had one child, a daughter named Deirdre. A druid said that she would grow up to be the most beautiful woman in Ireland; but, he said, her beauty would bring trouble, sorrow and bloodshed to many. In an effort to avoid this, her father sent her to be brought up by a foster-mother in a hut in a secluded spot. Food was brought to them, but Deirdre was allowed to see no one from the outside world. In this way she was sheltered until she was fourteen. Then, one night, a hunter lost his way and sought hospitality at their hut. The hunter was reluctantly taken in by the foster-mother; she was afraid that the secret of the presence of the girl would now be out. The hunter was astonished by the girl's beauty. He thought that she would be a suitable wife for King Conchobar, and at the first opportunity he told the King all about her.

The King decided to go to see for himself, and he fell in love with her and proposed marriage; but she asked for a year and a day to make up her mind. The King granted this.

Meanwhile, one day, Deirdre saw three of the most handsome men in Ireland. They were singing as they walked. She was fascinated by them, and she fell in love with Naoise, who was taller than the others. He returned her love, and Deirdre fled with the men, who were brothers. Eventually they came to Scotland and gave a help to the king of that country. But the King of Scotland also wanted Deirdre for himself. At length she and the three brothers retired to a very secluded spot to live in peace.

Meanwhile King Conchobar said at a great feast that he missed the sons of Usnach (the brothers) and wanted them to return. His words were sweet, but there was no kind intention in his heart. He asked Fergus to find them and Deirdre and send them to him at Emain Macha.

Fergus travelled to Scotland, but Deirdre was very troubled by Fergus's arrival. She was full of doubts about returning to live in Ireland, but Naoise wished to return, and he brushed aside her fears. On the way back to Ireland, Deirdre wished to stay at Rathlin Island; but Naoise would not listen, and they landed in Ireland upon the rock of Usnach. King Borach (a friend of King Conchobar) greeted them with a feast, but Fergus was in a dilemma: he wanted to protect the four he had brought to Ireland, but he was under a solemn oath to accept the hospitality. He stayed for the feast, and sent his two sons forward to protect them, but Fergus was betrayed. One of his sons tried to help, but the other had been bribed. The sons of Usnach were murdered at Armagh, and Deirdre committed suicide through grief.

Fergus was furious at this betrayal of his honour, and he raised an army that destroyed Emain Macha. Conchobar was cursed so that none of his descendants would succeed to the throne.

H. Browne wrote in a poem that as he walked by the Dun a shadow fell across the sun and a cool wind blew in his face, for Deirdre of the Sorrows was passing by. Nearby is an ancient fort, called Doonfort, and a chambered cairn.

There are three small loughs. Lough na Crannog with its ancient lake-dwelling in the middle is enchanting. The others are Lough Dhu ('the dark lough') and Lough Fad ('the long lough'). Here the landscape was shaped by ancient glaciers, which scraped their way over the landscape in the Ice Age.

Marconi's Cottage lies at the end of the shore, and it is often thought that wireless experiments were carried out here; in fact, the experiments were carried out in a house in the town.

Old coal seams can be seen, and salt pans where salt was once extracted.

The chief exports of the region today are perhaps dulse (an edible seaweed) and yellow man (a hard yellow toffee) – not to mention lots of lovely fish!

The waters of the Sea of Moyle (North Channel) have long been associated with the Legend of the Children of Lir. Lir was chieftain of the Tuatha Dé Danann, a tribe that lived in Ireland long ago, but his wife died after a sickness of three nights. Soon after this, his friend Bodb Dearg, King of the Tuatha Dé Danann, feeling sorry for Lir, asked him to come and choose a new wife from his three foster-daughters. He chose Aodh and she bore him two children, but she later died giving birth to twin sons. The children were Fionnuala, Aodh, Fiachra and Conn. Lir was overcome with grief, but again his friend had a solution: he offered Aodh's sister, Aoife, for a wife.

Aoife did honour to her sister's children, but gradually she became jealous and she was determined to be rid of them. She placed them in a chariot and drove away to quiet spot; then she told her attendants to kill them, but they refused. She had not the courage to kill them herself, so she took them to the Lake of the Oaks, and there turned them into four swans, white and beautiful. This was the spell: they were to remain swans until the Woman from the South and the Man from the North came together, after they had spent 300 years on Lough Dairbhreach, 300 years on Sruth na Maoile between Ireland and Scotland and 300 years at Domnann and Inis Gluaire. She said that they could keep their own speech, and that they could sing the sweetest music in the entire world.

Lir missed his children, so he went in search of them. He arrived at Lough Dairbhreach, where they were living. Fionnuala told him what had happened, and Lir was broken-hearted.

The swans lived out their enchanted life, and people came from all around to listen to their music. Sruth na Maoile was a fierce, wild sea for the swans, and they were often swept away by great storms, but they always reunited at the Rock of the Seals. After 300 years they went to Inis Gluaire, and Christianity seems to have arrived at the island at this time.

St Mochaomhog, who lived there, came one day to the Lake of the Birds and saw the swans. He asked them if they were the children of Lir, and he said that he had come to the island for their sakes. At the time Lairgnen was King of Connaught, and Deoca of Munster was his wife. This was the meeting of the Man from the North and the Woman from the South. The Queen had heard about the swans, and she wanted them to entertain her, so her husband went to fetch them from the holy saint. However, Mochaomhog refused to give them up. At this, Lairgnen seized them from the altar, two in each hand; but as soon as he touched them they changed into three withered old men and one withered old woman.

Lairgnen ran away in terror, but Fionnuala spoke: "Come and baptize us now, for we are near death."

And so it happened. They were buried, Fionnuala in the middle, Conn on the right, Fiachra on her left and Aodh between her arms. A stone was placed over them and their names written in ogham. Their 300 years of wandering had come to an end.

In ancient days Ballycastle was called Margietown, and from Shane O'Neill's time, about 1565, the town was called Baile Caislein or the Town of Sorley Boy.

After James I had ensured by patent that the MacDonnells were the lords of all of North Antrim, grants of land were made by Sir Randal MacDonnell to one Hugh O'Neill on 9 November 1612; but Sir Randal and his wife reserved the right to come to live at Ballycastle. They built a castle on the site of the former castle, which had given the town its name. The eastern gable of the castle remained until 1848, when it was considered to be dangerous.

In 1734 Ballycastle had sixty-two householders: sixteen

Catholics, thirty-two Anglicans, and fourteen Presbyterians.

Rose McNeill, a descendant of Hugh O'Neill, married Hugh Boyd, the Rector of Romoan. Their son, Hugh Boyd, in 1734 obtained a lease of the collieries, and in 1736 he obtained a deed for the village of Ballycastle. He was a great benefactor of the town, and soon made it a wealthy place with many industries – salt and soap manufacturers, an ironworks, weavers, tanners, a glass factory and a brewery.

Recently the old glass factory was uncovered near the mouth of the Margy River, and the remains of dark-green beer bottles were found. The industry was established in 1755, mainly producing bottles. There are also some panes of glass in the old windows of Holy Trinity Church in the Diamond which are thought by some to be Ballycastle glass.

The original little harbour of Ballycastle was at Port Brittas, and this was reconstructed by Mr Boyd. When he died in 1765 the town had twenty vessels employed in trade.

As a youngster I can remember a view of Rathlin Island and the Antrim Hills, which rolled down to the North Channel and the Atlantic. Rathlin has always been a 'separate' place. In the Middle Ages it belonged to Scotland. It is only thirteen miles from Campbeltown and the Mull of Kintyre. Moira O'Neill has written a poem called 'The Rachray Man', in which she says that she would marry a Rathlin man. Her lover would not listen to reason or rhyme, for he was trying to hurry her as best he could. He was destined to live on the island along with her. Rathlin lay beyond her in the bay. There was fishing and fighting, and what did the people of the island care? She might have taken Peter from over the hill, a poacher and a kind poor boy. There were sea caves, filled by the waves. She would never win back whatever might fall, so she prayed for good luck, for they would see her no more. An island man was the main mischief and she had never been married before. She cried out as she thought of her fate when they danced at the fair, for in Rathlin, or Rachray, there was no Christianity.

When I think about Rathlin Island, I think of Bruce and his spider in a cave. On the island there is a cave known as Bruce's Cave, and there are also the remains of an old castle. It was in the stable of this castle that the Scots king took refuge, trying to recover after his defeat in battle. He decided never to give up as he watched the spider with determination weaving its web. From then on he was able to overcome his enemies.

Rathlin is a bird watchers' paradise. There are Manx shearwaters, fulmars, petrels, buzzards, peregrines and many other rare birds, including choughs.

There were once two princesses from Isla who got into trouble while staying on the island. They tried to escape back to their own land, but they were transformed into two great rocks.

Chapter 9

The Glensmen

The Glens of Antrim consist of the Barony of Glenarm and part of Carey. They lie within what was the ancient kingdom of Dalriada. According to tradition, Dalriada stretched from the River Bush to the Finneachta. It is quite likely that the early inhabitants of Dalriada were Irish Picts of Cruithin, who were akin to the Picts of Northern Scotland. Dalriada is named after Cairbre Riada, whose father, Conaire II, King of Ireland, was slain in AD 220. Dal means 'descendants of'. In St Patrick's time the twelve sons of Erc, who was fourth in descent from Cairbre, controlled Dalriada, and a few colonies already established in Alba (Scotland).

Fergus was the youngest of these sons. He received Patrick with kindness, and as a result he earned a great blessing. He headed an expedition to Scotland with his brothers Loarn and Aongus about AD 500, and they firmly established the kingdom of Dalriada.

Kenneth MacAlpin conquered the entire kingdom of the Picts in AD 842, becoming king of the whole of Scotland. From this line the House of Stuart and the present British royal family are descended.

The descendants of Fergus and his family continued to rule Dalriada, but they were somewhat weakened by the advance of the Scottish kingdom. They were overcome eventually by the tribes of the Clan Colla, the Ui Tuirtre and Fir-Li.

When surnames came into existence in the tenth century, we do not know which ones were taken by the old rulers of the Cairbre Riada. O'Flinn and O'Linn and O'Donnell were prominent names of the Ui Tuirtre. McLevy and Ui Tuirtre are derived from a commander of the Uluti, who helped the Fir-Li and Ui Tuirtre against the O'Cathans or O'Kanes from Tyrone, but they were defeated.

After the English invasion, the Earls of Ulster owned Dalriada; and when King John came to Carrickfergus to put down the rebellion of De Lacy, he gave Dalriada to Alan, Earl of Galloway, who died in 1234. The lands must then have reverted to the Earls of Ulster. Patrick, son of Thomas of Galloway was murdered at Haddington in 1242; and when John Bisset and Walter (his uncle) were accused, they fled to Ireland, where they obtained the Glens from the Earl of Ulster, de Burgh. From this John, the Bissets were known as MacEoin ('the son of John'). McKeown is another version of the name. A condition was placed on the two that they would join the Crusades to the Holy Land and never return, but instead of proceeding to Jerusalem they started life anew in the holy land of Ireland.

The McQuillans are thought to have come from Wales, but they rose to become chiefs of Dalriada. Some think the name McQuillan is derived from the Welsh Llewellyn. The McQuillans are thought first to have settled in Connaught, where they are mentioned in the ancient Annals. Later the McQuillans were overthrown by the O'Donnells. The O'Kanes were opponents of the McQuillans.

There were several branches of the O'Kanes, known as Clan Manus. Some of them assumed the name McHenry. In 1542 the O'Kanes, with McSweeney, helped to defeat the combined McQuillan and MacDonnell army. The Battle of Aura in 1583 at last established the MacDonnells as Lords of the Glens.

The McAulas were a Scots family from Dumbartonshire. They received lands in the Larne region from Sir James Knockinsay. The O'Donnellys were another Kinnel-Owen tribe who aided the O'Kanes. The O'Haras were brought by the de Burghs from Connaught, and they settled around Loughguile. The McSporrans or McSparrans were also a Scottish Highland tribe.

McKillop is another Glens name, and McKillops were numerous in Glenballyeamon.

At a later date the MacDonnells either fought with the O'Neills or made peace with them. Sorley Boy was one of their foremost chieftains. At one time Elizabeth I sent Sorley some letters which belonged to the Bissets. He wanted the entire tract from Larne to Bushmills, after assisting Elizabeth against the O'Neills. Tradition states that Sorley Boy placed the letters on the point of his sword and exclaimed that it would be by the sword he would hold his lands, not by the Queen's writ.

From the top of Glendun it is possible to see the great spread of Orra mountain. Here was fought the great Battle of Aura (Orra) in July 1583, between the McQuillans and O'Neills on one side and the MacDonnells on the other. The MacDonnells ruled the Moinnavan Bog, which lay between Tievebulliagh and Trostan, and many of the enemy rushed into it and perished. The locals told of finding pikes and muskets here for years afterwards. The battle raged down the entire valley of Glenshesk. The MacDonnells were victorious, and celebrations were held on top of Trostan. A memorial cairn was built on the mountain in honour of Sorley Boy, the MacDonnell leader. Two graves on Orra are said to be those of Hugh Phelim O'Neill and his servant.

Phelimy Roe's Cairn is in the centre of the townland of Altaveedan, about half a mile south-east of the road from Armoy to Clogh. It is said that some of his letters were scraped on stone as he lay dying.

The result of the Battle of Aura was that estates and castles belonging to the McQuillans of the Route passed to the MacDonnells.

After this battle a saying arose that a rush bush was never known to deceive anyone but a McQuillan. McQuillan retired from North Antrim, and he is said to have lived in a cell in the Abbey of Layde, where he died at a great age.

However, the poet Dusty Rhodes thought otherwise. Say, he said, hear you the tidings, Mor, or did he see the signals from the shore of many of their kinsmen that would land at Torr, and the standard was raised on the heights of Torcor. McQuillan had sworn that his fair sister would no longer mourn. With lance and with sabre they made havoc and flame. MacDonnell, the haughty, had come to Aura with many weapons that included a drum. With an insult the knave had dared fight McQuillan, the brave. McQuillan had summoned his clans to the fight, his best and bravest, from mountain and brae, from Inishowen's headlands to level Armoy. Reaching to the sky was Dunseverick Castle and steep Ballintoy.

They came from the hillsides, they came from the shore and they came from the hillside of distant Altmore. From valley and corrie, from many mountains, they came in fury and might. They came as the torrent leaps down on the rock, and they came as an eagle sweeps down on the flock. They came as the billows dash furious and free, where the fury of the storm is spent on the sea. There are tall battle spears from the Foyle and the Bann, and mountaineers from the vale of Glenaan. There were sons from far Donegal, the land of the clouds, to ride beside McQuillan the Proud. A number of them passed from the shore, and McQuillan was proud of them as he went into the battle with their clans. Did anyone hear the battle shock as it burst forth on the ground? There were spear thrusts and sabre strokes, ruin and death: unshriven and neglected the stricken lay dejected. It was a holocaust, and Donagha Mor was mad with battle lust and drunk with gore. They killed many, and they asked for no mercy. In the halls of Dunluce Castle there was mirth and merriment. In the halls of Dunluce loud voices rang and there were wailings of sorrow. The bravest shall lie in the dawn together, beneath the blue sky amongst the heather. They were unburied and stark in their fields of slaughter. Maidens cried out for them, fond fathers mourned them. He had fought the good fight, but he had fought in vain. MacDonnell had conquered, McQuillan was slain. He was killed by a shaft from the armies of MacCaura, and he died that day on the red field of Aura.

Near our own time, and loosely associated with the Glens, is the Clan MacDonnell.

Colla MacDonnell was an older brother of Sorley Boy, and he was the third son of Alexander MacIan Cathanac MacDonnell, Lord of Islay, Kintyre and the Glens and great-grandson of John, Lord of the Isles. By his marriage in 1399 with Margery, heiress of the McKeowns, John obtained the Lordship of the Glens, or the eastern part of the County Antrim from Larne to the Bush River. Alexander arrived in the Glens about 1500, and he is thought to have built Dunaneanie Castle at Ballycastle. Alexander's six sons were James, Angus, Colla, Alexander, Sorley Boy and Donnell Gorme.

Sir James of Kintyre succeeded his father, taking over his Scottish estates. He appointed Colla Lord of the Glens under him. Colla built Kinbane Castle (Ballycastle) between 1545 and 1547. He married Eveleen, a daughter of McQuillan, Lord of North Antrim.

The Route of North Antrim is generally considered to embrace the Baronies of Carey, Dunluce and Kilconway and the Liberty of Coleraine.

Colla later laid claim to the lands of the Route, and disputes continued after his death until Sorley Boy defeated the McQuillans at the Battle of Aura. It is thought that Colla was buried in Bun-na-Margie monastery, but many of his descendants are buried in Layde Old Churchyard.

Direct descendants of Colla through the male line are still to be found in the Glens.

In 1620, Randal, son of Sorley Boy, was created Earl of Antrim. The descendants of Sorley Boy and Randal MacDonnell are still Earls of Antrim, descended through the male line since the eighteenth century. The MacDonnell coat of arms can be seen in Craighagh Church, and also on several tombstones in Layde, Bun-na-Margie and elsewhere.

The McAllisters, a sub-clan of the MacDonnells, were brought from Scotland as support, many of them settling in the Route. The MacDonnells of Antrim are a leading branch of the Scots Clan Donnell, and as such they rank amongst the most distinguished representatives of the present Clan Colla. Domhnaill (pronounced Donnell) is the original form of the name.

The Lia Fail (the Stone of Fate) is said to have been brought to Ireland by the Tuatha Dé Danann. According to legend the stone was taken by the Irish to Scotland, where King Kenneth MacAlpin placed it at Scone. On it is written, 'Should fate not fail, wherever this stone should be found, the Scots monarchs of the realm should be found.' The stone rested for many years under the Coronation Chair at Westminster Abbey, but it has now been returned to Scotland.

Most Scottish clans had their individual war cries. After a period of silence they launched themselves into the attack. The MacDonnell war cry was *Fraoch eilen* (Heathery Island). The badge of the MacDonnells and the McAllisters was the *fraoch gorm* (the common heath).

It is possible to trace the Lords of the Isles back to Fergus, who with his warriors founded the Scots Kingdom of Dalriada, the parent kingdom being Dalriada in North Antrim. He was descended from the Irish King Conaire.

The Plantations of the seventeenth century did not seem to affect the Glens, though Queen Elizabeth wanted to give 'Burney Dall' (Cushendall) to Henry Knowles, vice-chamberlain and Treasurer of her Household. Some think that from the prevalence of Scots names from the sixteenth century, some dispossession must have taken place. At any rate, the names McAuley and McAllister became common. The clan fights that characterized the sixteenth century appear to have largely died out, and the area became peaceful.

From old records we can obtain a glimpse of what life was like in the Glens in the eighteenth and nineteenth centuries. The Reverend Stewart Dobbs, writing about the parish in 1806, described the people and their way of life. There were 119 Protestant families and 511 Roman Catholic families in the parish. The main foods were oatmeal, potatoes, milk, fish and some wheat. The houses were cabins built out of stone with thatched roofs. The fireplace was at the gable end of the house. Typically, there were two rooms lighted by two small windows. On the whole the people were healthy, but tuberculosis was prevalent. Irish was the main language, and ploughs, harrows and spades were the main farming tools. On stony ground a spade known as a *kib* was used.

The slide car (or slipe), a form of wheelless cart for use on mountainsides, was used. The County Antrim variety differs from others in that 'shoes' (wooden protectors) covered the ends of the shafts trailing on the ground. These were replaceable when worn out. The four-wheeled box car, or wheel car, was popular, and until recent times almost every farm had one. They served for all purposes.

The inhabitants of Layd were thought to be shrewd, cunning folk, with a great reputation for hospitality. They had little interest in travelling abroad, and consequently many remained at home. Many were idle for nearly half a year, when crops could not be grown. Many of the men went to sea for a number of years and then returned home, and it is said that many of them knitted stockings in winter.

Kelp was burned along the shore, and stacked in oblong pits lined with stone when dry. The kelp formed a hard cake when burned. Some of it went to Coleraine and Larne, and some was shipped to Liverpool.

Potatoes used to be planted near the coast. A piece of land on the mountainside was given to each family.

Salmon spawned in the river, and the fry left in April, when they weighed only about two ounces. When they returned in June, always from the south, in shoals, they were from four to eight pounds each. The River Acre was noted for good trout, but most of the rivers had a good supply. Offshore, lythe, turbot, mullet, mackerel, herring, lobsters and crabs were plentiful.

The heather-covered mountains provided game.

Potatoes, oats, barley and flax were grown, and the area suited the small black cattle which were raised for beef. There also used to be a stocky breed of pony, mostly grey with a broad back and short legs, but they have now completely died out.

Booleying was the name given to the practice of heading for the mountains for the summer to graze cattle. They went up in about May and returned in about October, when there would be great celebrations at Halloween for the reunion. Up in the hills they built little shelters of sods and stone and thatched them with heather. Ballyvooley is a townland whose name refers to the custom, and Tievebulliagh means 'the mountain of *booleying*'.

Butter was made. It was stored for long periods in wooden casks buried in bogs. Old casks are still sometimes found in the bogs.

In Cushendall there were eight annual fairs held between 14 February and the 23 December, but there was no weekly market. The town and the surrounding area were well supplied with corn mills and flax mills.

Cushendall was also a post town. In the early nineteenth century a car with the mail from Glenarm arrived in Cushendall every morning at nine o'clock. On its arrival, a car took the mail for Ballycastle, returning to Cushendall in time for the next day's delivery. The fare from Cushendall to Glenarm was one shilling and to Ballycastle it was one shilling and sixpence.

At one time a steamer used to call at Cushendall on its way from Larne to Glasgow. Also small vessels plied between Cushendall and Belfast, but Ballymena was the main town where the Glens folk went on special shopping expeditions.

The poet H. Browne wrote that a journey was undertaken every fortnight to the town of Ballymena to bring home the yellow meal and other essentials, for the people had large appetites. One week on a Saturday, as he was heading home again, a warm April sun was shining from the sky. The leaf was on the elm and the blossom on the blackthorn, and the yellow birds were warblin' and maybe so was the poet. He had sold a heifer and got a fair price for her. The dealers tried to beat him down, but he persisted to obtain his price, and now he had the bacon, and syrup, and the brandy balls, also the biscuits and the treacle, the sugar and the tea.

Near Cargan there was a little plantation of trees known as Ben's

Plantin', and in this region highwaymen held up travellers and farmers returning home from Ballymena after selling their wares.

There was some sort of coast road from an early date, and in 1633 Richard Dobbs wrote about the difficulty of travelling in the Glens. The main route was over the headlines to Red Bay, and it was useful to have a guide. The route was very dangerous in winter. The road between Red Bay and Cushendun was a very difficult one. In the late 1830s the great Glendun Viaduct was built. It stands with tall, graceful arches spanning the glen and the Dun River. It was a great place for spectacular firework displays. It became known as the Big Bridge.

Glendun Viaduct.

Another great feat of engineering was the building of the narrow-gauge railway. This opened in the 1870s to transport minerals from mines in the Glens. One line went to Red Bay via Glenariff, and the other went from Ballymena to Parkmore – an isolated place on the top of the mountain. The railway proved a blessing for many travellers, especially in winter when there were often heavy falls of snow. Many travellers came to the Glens at Christmas, and they must have missed the beautiful scenery while they were away. Today Parkmore is a deserted village, and the narrow-gauge railway no longer functions, but in its heyday it was a wonder.

Siobhan ni Luain has written about the narrow-gauge line: Looking up through the trees, leaning out from the door, he shall never again see the train from Parkmore with its small whining engine yet sturdy and grand as it wound its way through the land. There was once a time when the train like the river was part of the Glen. It was not possible to predict what the train might be bringing to the halt, but there were bushes with the birds singing. There was a small smoky train that rumbled like thunder. No one would be running again to stand on the bridge and see the small train leap straight at the darkness and thunder beneath and out and away to the wind. No child would wait now to feel the bridge shake, or to shout for adventure's sweet dangerous sake. Where the silver rail shone there was wilderness now, and the whins, the wild ash and the weed grasses now grow. When she was a child she saw the train running just the same as the river, but the world was in a hurry and it had little use for a narrow-gauge line.

The part of the moor where the main Ballycastle road starts its long upward climb is known as Granny's in the Glen. Here a long, sturdy, whitewashed farmhouse stands on its bed of gravel. It was aptly named Caiseal(na)grine ('rock of the sun'), but now it is called Castlegreen. In the past the time could be calculated from the sun's rays on a rock in the garden. Now the garden is noted for its daffodils and roses. There was a shop here: petrol was sold and wool bought. Here one came for coal, tobacco, scythes and flour, ladies' stays and men's boots and papers. The shop was a kaleidoscope of colour forty years ago, just before modern ideas took root. Dogs basked in the sun in the middle of the road and sparks flew from the boots of the men with scythes as they marched down the road to cut the hay.

If the weather was bad, the shepherds of the Glens had to walk over the mountains for long hours to rescue their flocks from deep snowdrifts. Their faithful collies were their only helpers.

Primroses bloomed in the Glens.

When summer came the hay had to be harvested. The work was hard in those difficult times before tractors. Hard at work, lapping, tossing and rucking, the young men stripped to the waist in the hot sun, but the older men kept themselves well covered. Sometimes a straw hat replaced the paddy one during the summer. Foxgloves, bucky rozes, fuchsia and honeysuckle grew in profusion in the hedges and fields.

The turf that had been cut in the early summer had to be brought home or stacked on the mountain. This involved many days away. Tea was made on turf fires, and sweet water was drawn from places amongst the rocks, which were almost hidden under a layer of fine turf dust. Turf was carried in large slatted baskets until the men's arms ached. All the time people hoped to find something exciting in the bog – for example, a butter cask from long ago, or the antlers of an Irish elk.

In the autumn, harvest thanksgivings were held in the little churches. Glorious rowans, haws and juicy blackberries were picked. The hills were purple with heather.

In winter the glens folk enjoyed some leisure. There were dances and ceilidhs – old-fashioned dances as well as modern dances. The men took out their guns and in the red sunsets brought home their game – rabbits, snipe, grouse, woodcock and the odd pheasant. Women knitted and made quilts with their friends. And they gossiped! There was plenty of crack around the log-and-turf fires on the winter nights, while the wind howled and the crickets sounded. There would be tales of deals, fairs and animals, of fairy thorns and some grand concert. A song might be sung, a verse, joke or a riddle repeated. A draw on the pipe was grand. Holly was gathered from the bare hills, and Christmas trees were cut down.

Dancing has always been a favourite pastime in the Glens, and farm kitchens were the first dance halls. A space would be cleared and the family and their friends would dance and sing. The men's boots struck sparks from the flagged floor as they danced the four-hand reel or the lancers, usually to the music of the fiddle.

In some families, dancing was prevalent for almost fifty years. In the 1920s a family dance hall was built at Castlegreen, and until the Troubles it was a place of merriment for people from all parts of Ulster. In the beginning the family provided the music: the sisters played the piano and one brother played the violin. The postman joined them, for he was good at the accordion. At length the hall became a venue for top showbands, and the dancing became almost entirely 'pop'. The original oil lamps were replaced by the latest flashing lights associated with discotheques.

Siobhan ni Luain has written about springtime: When she was young she might steal away to pass from the Head Ditch across the last good grass where the hill called the mountain spread its friendly challenges above the head. She loved to climb, to follow in the footsteps of the sheep. From oasis to oasis the turning tracks would climb the mountainside until they came to where they last grass died, where tumbled stone was piled on tumbled stone. There she would be in the wilderness, a tall thin girl in a pretty dress. She was the sole created princess of the land. Arms pressed back against a ledge of stone, in the great rock behind her, but she was not alone, for beneath her lay the painted valley with all the little houses that she knew. The sun that shone in her childhood took delight in spending itself on walls washed white. She would listen to the peewit's cry, the curlew's call. The little ledge was the spring's first call. Small rivers join the main river down below. She could climb now, for it was not so very steep, thanks to the activities of the sheep, which rested where she once stood with the wind blowing around her like a flood. She saw strange seabirds seeking seas unknown. It was wise to wait until sunset to watch the circle of the dreaming hills.

Maureen Donnelly has written about the Cushendall Farmhouse. She was lucky enough to know Robert Hyndman, one of the sons who lived with his family in this old farmhouse. The building has since been moved from Cushkib, overlooking Red Bay, to its new home at the Folk Museum at Cultra, County Down. Robert Hyndman and Maureen Donnelly had many conversations about the life and times of his family. His father at one time had a famous greyhound called Donal, which had not fared too well at the start and had to be kept in the parents' big bed; it lived to become one of the most famous dogs in the Glens. The words of a song by James Delargy can be fitted to the tune of 'Master McGra'. The song is called 'Dan Hyndman's Greyhound'. The greyhound, it states, was born in Cushkib. It was deep in the heart, it was short on the rib, and the jaws were brown. The hound had a stumpy tail. The dog had a fine pedigree, and it was owned by a man name Magee. Its mother was sported around Tiveragh, and one could trace its ancestors to Master McGra. The people of the town were all for sport – there was Stevenson, McKillop, McDermot and Mort. With their dogs on the slips they set out for the town and the best dog amongst them was Hyndman's greyhound. They hunted on Nappin right up to Magore, and there were many opportunities to kill game. Now the keepers of Aura, brave Willie and Hugh, had heard about the poachers; and when the boys saw them coming they started to run, and they gave them the slip on the slopes of Glendun. There were the two Courtneys, Ray and McFall. McClintock was coming but was held back by the fog, who gave Hyndman the word to watch his good dog. Now the meeting proceeded, and brave Hugh took the chair, for if they did not act quickly they would not leave them a hare. He had a bill handy. Ray drew first, and his cut was long. Hugh drew next and his cut was also long. Willie drew next but his cut was small, but the smallest of all fell to McFall.

McFall got ready and assumed a disguise, and he was booted and coated from his toes to his eyes. He put on his sleeve waistcoat that had been made at Broughshane, and it was lined with sheepskin to keep out the rain. A chart was got ready, and he was to pass by Tievebulliagh and down by Maroo. He was to starboard a point, when reaching the town, in the hope that it would finish Dan Hyndman's greyhound. When he reached Cushkib most of them were in bed, and the lights were out, and the cattle were fed. He placed his parcel close to the wall when he heard a voice saying, "How are you, McFall?" What had brought them this night so far from his bog? Did his master send you here to destroy my good dog? He called his sons, who were hearty and strong, and they sent McFall fast along with two sticks. Now Dan kept his dog until it was quite old, and he sold it to a man in Belfast, who treated him well, but the keepers remembered Dan Hyndman's greyhound.

The people of the Glens were, and still are, great storytellers, and many an interesting tale has been spun about the Hyndman hearth. There was, however, little food and drink to give strangers. Times were hard, and the Glens folk found it hard to provide for their own families.

There was little poteen-making going on at this time. It was more common later on, but a large number of carts rattled past Hyndman's gate, and some of the main ingredients for poteen were hidden under some straw. Ingredients were simple – bran, treacle, yeast and brown sugar.

The tales told at the ceilidhs were also interesting, and at times they could be frightening. Tiveragh (the fairy hill) was too close for comfort. Just across the road was a well, but it was almost impossible to persuade an animal to drink the water. There were fairies – hundreds of them. There was one young fellow, Johnny Flanagan, who pastured his cattle in Glendun. The fairies got him, and it was six weeks before he returned. He never grew after this experience. A wee girl from up Glenaan way was just thirteen years of age when the fairies took her. She went away for a while, but when she returned she was lame.

Robert Hyndman also saw the fairies. He had been at his girlfriend's house up Glenaan, and was returning late one Easter Sunday night when he saw the entire place lit up by fairy lights. They were all over Tiveragh, all up Glenaan, and everywhere he looked. He was fortunate to reach home that night.

The people of the Glens were superstitious in the old days. One had only to look into a byre to see red yarn on the cows' and goats' horns.

There is a story about an old man called Randal who could 'place the blink' on anything. There was one old mare that he could not stand the sight of. One day he and the man that owned the mare were travelling down the road, and all of a sudden the mare lay down and died. The man that owned her rounded on Randal. He was mad with rage. He threatened Randal and compelled him to 'take off the blink' then and there. The mare arose, lively as ever, gave the harness a good shake and away they went.

Katie McGreer was another who was good at charms. She was also good at 'taking off the blink'. Dan, the father, had an old sow lying in the kitchen. She would have eaten her own piglets if they had come near her, and some of them were starving to death for she would not allow them to suckle. Dan's wife begged him to go to Katie for a charm, and he went reluctantly. He was not halfway before the sow rolled over and started to grunt. She allowed the piglets to take her milk, and that was the end of the matter.

On another occasion Robert was away on the mountain shooting. He tripped in a hole and twisted his ankle. It swelled to a great degree, but he managed to limp as far as the pub for a drink and a rest. The ankle swelled until it broke his bootlaces. It was very painful for a number of days, and he was helped on to his horse and sent to Katie for a charm. She uttered the charm and tied red yarn around his ankle; and by the time Robert reached home, he was able to jump down off the horse without feeling pain. The swelling had disappeared.

Skeoghs, or fairy thorns, were held in veneration, and very few would interfere with them. However, one fell in Henry Dan's field and he thought it a bit of easy-got fuel for his fire. He chopped up the wood and took it home. His wife placed some of the logs on the fire, but the next minute she swore that blood ran out of them, and she would use no more.

Another neighbour, Patrick McVicker, cut down a *skeogh* in his field. His wife became paralysed and could not speak for the next thirty years.

There is also a tale told about Margaret Hyndman, Robert's mother. One day one of the boys was coming through the garden gate, and he stood aside whilst she passed in front of him. She preceded him into the house, and he followed behind. When he passed through the door he was amazed to see his mother at the kitchen table up to her elbows in flour. She was baking.

He asked her, "Mother, how did you get in here?" For she had just come in from the garden.

She explained, "You must have seen my daylight wraith."

This meant that she might live long. Margaret Hyndman lived to the age of ninety-seven.

Halloween was an important time at Cushkib, and it was the time of the Cushkib Fair. On Halloween night, old and young from all parts gathered to play games and dance. Many a young couple was paired off here, and also many black eyes were acquired. There were all the usual games, like ducking for apples. There was also fortune-telling. If a boy wanted to know what was going on, he went to his girlfriend's house and placed two long nuts on a warm part of the hearth. When they were brown and tasty a lighted match was applied to each. If the flames swirled round from the boy's head to the girl's this was a signal for putting an arm round her.

Another popular game was 'Who's got the button?' – a guessing game. If a boy in the middle of a circle guessed right, he could claim a kiss from the girl of his choice.

Halloween was also a time for playing tricks and jokes on the neighbours – like removing their doors and gates and blaming it on the fairies!

Cushkib Fair was a popular occasion for the Hyndman family, for

106

their house was the centre of all the fun. Dan, the father, was a jolly fellow. He had a game played with five spoons. Four were hidden anywhere in the house, but the fifth was placed in the hearth so it was well burnt. The victim would spot it sticking out the hearth and tried to grab it. At this, Dan would laugh loudly and the poor fellow would be crying out round the kitchen with the pain of the burn.

The family had another game: 'Tilda's game'. Tilda and a partner were blindfolded and given a plate each. Both were told there was soot on the plate, and they were called upon to see what kind of a mess they could make of their partner. However, only Tilda's had soot; the other plate might have flour. Tilda usually made a real mess of the other person!

On Easter Monday there was another important gathering for some fun – especially amongst the young people. It was on this day that competitors rolled eggs down Tiveragh – and some of them rolled the girls as well, if they had the chance! The eggs were dyed with whin blossom.

It is said that there are still long-legged Hyndmans in the Glens.

John Hewitt has written about Cushkib Fair: One gable of the Hyndmans' house lay before the road, one towards the slope that meets the shoulder of the storied hill. The door faced east, well out of the wind. There were sparse trees about it and walls. There was also a quarry-pit and a burn across the road. The house was once a noisy family of tall sons, famous for their great deeds. There was horseplay with harness, ballads, dances and games. They probably knew that the acres were too few to hold them long.

There was a little group of houses high up on the hillside, and they were in ruins and deserted. This was a typical clachan of ancient days, where a group of mountain farmers had lived until the start of the nineteenth century. They were very poor and led very simple lives. It is possible to see a pigsty, a small shed that housed a cow or goat, a flat stone where the chickens were fed and the ruined houses whose roofs are now open to the sky. There are 'keeping holes' at either side of the large hearth where bits and pieces – like pins, thread and cord – were kept. A unique feature of these old houses is the method by which they were thatched. Old cattle bones were driven into spaces between the stones to make firm pegs, and the thatch was attached to these. Lying outside is the old *braidh* for grinding corn. This is a round, flat stone with a hole in the middle.

The grain was placed below on another flat stone, and a handle was attached by which the upper stone was turned and the grain was ground.

The people must have spoken Gaelic. They led a very simple life that has disappeared for ever. It is sad to see the fuchsias growing up the old chimneys and the sweet gooseberries growing wild in the garden. The garden and the potato patch must have been shared in this little community. It is thought that two Miss MacDonnells were the last inhabitants.

The Glens folk were, above all, individualists. This was perhaps due to the hard way of life on those lonely hillside farms. The men had to be strong-minded and self-reliant as well as physically fit. Eccentrics, however, were tolerated for the light relief they brought to the people.

Sometimes an old fellow came to the little shop once a week with a big sack for his groceries, and he lived alone far up the glen. He had a rather long thumbnail on his right hand, and, when asked why he kept it so long, he replied that he kept it for peeling potatoes. On another farm lived two brothers and their sister, and every night they held a ritual. The sister had to bake a scone – a soda farl – to eat before they went to bed. A boy with a reputation for being mean would greet his visitors with the offer that he would make them tea.

Many houses had a big open turf fire and a crane or crook from which was suspended a big black pot or kettle. One old lady boiled potatoes in a large three-legged pot, and she fixed a cow's horn over one leg to hold the potatoes in the pot as she drained them off. Many of the Glens folk drained potatoes into the street outside their doors.

Sam Henry, the folklorist, mentioned some old names for dishes in the Ballycastle area. Sowans was the traditional supper for Candlemas Eve and Halloween. It consisted of oatmeal, buttermilk and berries.

One well-known song describes a typical mountain farmer. The song is based on a poem by John Hewitt: he had a generous field of potatoes, and he also had a great field of oats. There was a little bit of clover grass to help feed the goats. There was a stall for feeding them, and there was a still for making whiskey. There were cows amongst the grass, a billy goat and an ass.

Also by John Hewitt there is a poem called 'Haymaking in the

Low Meadow': The rain stayed off and they would let the wind dry the hay. Each year, when the fields were safely stacked, the hay would lie in dark bundles day by day. It was necessary to perform piecemeal spurts of work because of the mounting tide of duties – pulling, dubbing, cutting the ripe corn, or drawing turf. It was also good to have some days free from rain or only light showers. Before the corn was ready they took a chance: it was Sunday and the afternoon. Earth's needs were foremost and older, and the Masses were heard in the mornings. A tall farmer came with his leaping dogs and was tending his sheep. They rose at his orders, and lifted the laps and dropped them into a circled heap. They trampled and turned on the rick. His brother stabbed and twisted, hoisted and carried high his burden in its proper place, and stabbed again, until the occasion arose. The other man, with defter help, had beaten them and already had a new foundation spread. There was not much talk that day. Silence prevailed, for who could work with others and hold his tongue? There would be a slow laden conversation, that on a dry day gives to every piece of hay or oats the word that must be said, the proverbs picked from hedge and bush. It was the fourth year they had laboured here in the same fields. He knew what to expect, for there was little change from field to field and hardly any change from year to year. The rain was not too far away to let the ritual continue. Already on his forearms and brow the sweat beads gathered. When the fourth rick was bound it was the end. They passed to reach the gate and the rain glistened, but they would have to wait.

De Blacam wrote a piece called 'A Glensman Speaks'. He wrote that the people of the plain country inland and down into the province of Leinster were good folk, but when they wanted help with the harvest or any other hard work they called upon the study breed that came from the hills. The people of the hills breed are strong and able, and they could go to the mountains. The little huts up there housed able-bodied men, workers and great thinkers. High up in the mountain, in the quiet places, one sees the giants that must be priests or soldiers. The higher one went the more able is the manhood, and the fairer are the quiet-eyed maidens.

A little man with a big pipe said, "Excuse me for interrupting," and he asked where they had come from.

"The home where he was brought up", said the big speaker,

"was the little hut at the head of the glen."

The little man said that he thought as much, and he continued to smoke.

A townswoman praised the beautiful scenery, and she stepped out of an expensive saloon car to view the valley through an eyeglass on a handle.

"If you had to plough and dig the scenery, ma'am," said the man, "you would be content with less of it."

H. Browne wrote a poem called 'Andy Maguire': He sat by the fire but he was old now and tired easily. He was in need of a rest, but it was not too long that he had hair on his chest. He could handle the ploughing along with the others, but at ploughing and reaping or cutting the grass he was never known to be out of his class. He was known for his courting of the lasses, but now he was old and could court no more.

Sydney Bell wrote a poem entitled 'For the Ones Who Went Away'. His heart went out to the little homes that dotted the mountain, where clouds swirl down when the sun goes in, and the blue smoke greets the sky. With their thatch and the low half-door the wide-eyed children played, and the welcome light in the window waits for the ones who went away. The sea lies calm with the coming of the dawn as it crept down the hill. The larks rise high in the sky, and the morning then is brisk. The mother stirs to flame the smouldering peat that lit her eyes as she said a prayer for the ones that had gone away. Dear to her were the dark hills – as dear as the dewy glen where the blackthorn tree was a joy to see. But his heart went out to the little cottages below the rocks of grey where still the light of the window waits for the ones that went away.

Many people were forced to leave the Glens with the onset of the Great Famine in the mid-nineteenth century. One old lady in her ninety-fifth year told of the custom of 'convoying' – the practice whereby a crowd of friends and relations would accompany emigrants to the boat when they were leaving Ireland. Many went from Larne – usually to America. The party usually stayed at McNeill's Hotel the night before sailing. Dancing and singing went on into the early hours of the morning; at last only the closest relatives and the ones that were leaving were left in the room. Then the lamenting began. It was often the last time they would be together on God's earth. It was a very sad time – like death.

Since there were always comings and goings between Scotland and the north of Ireland, Gaelic Irish and the Scots language became somewhat fused. Odd Scottish words are still used in the Glens for everyday things, such as *fuuochs* for blackberries, and *braw*, meaning good or brave.

Rathlin Island has for many years been considered as part of the Glens. The island has a long history of its own, some of the best remembered parts being the saddest. In legend the island owes its origins to the mother of Finn MacCool, the great giant. It is said that Finn drained Ireland dry of whiskey, so his mother went to Scotland to try to obtain some there. She carried in her apron a number of trees to use as stepping stones. Less than halfway across she tripped and fell. She dropped her load, which formed Rathlin Island, and she was pinned underneath it. To this day, when a storm blows up it is said that the old witch is kicking.

Rathlin is situated strategically between Ireland and Scotland, and invaders often made it a stopping place. The island had its own chief, and it is said that the Danes caused much havoc trying to capture the island. Robert the Bruce, as we have seen, fled to Rathlin when things were going against him. Later, when his courage had been restored, he achieved success.

In 1551 Sorley Boy MacDonnell occupied Rathlin Island with his Highlanders. The Lord Deputy, Sussex, after the capture of Sorley Boy, sent four ships to take the island, but the English were repulsed. Only the commander survived. Later he was exchanged for Sorley. Sussex wreaked great vengeance on the islanders, and he slaughtered the entire garrison.

On 22 July 1575 there was yet another tragedy on the island. Sorley at this time spent most of his time with his family and the wives and children of his principal clansmen. They had brought their family treasures to the island for safety. A great slaughter took place, and Sorley Boy was distracted. He ran up and down the strand at Ballycastle, demented, powerless to help. It is estimated that at least 600 people lost their lives.

In 1642 the most terrible massacre of all took place: Charles I ordered the Earl of Argyll to take a large force to Ireland to subdue the rebels there. Rathlin was chosen as the first stop for the troops, but when they arrived and found the King's enemies there the entire population was put to the sword. It is said that many women were thrown into the sea. The cliffs where many women watched the battle were named the Hill of Screaming. The leader of the invasion was Duncan Campbell, and from that day the Campbell clan was not popular on Rathlin.

In 1565, Glentaisie was the scene of a terrible battle between the O'Neills and the MacDonnells. The O'Neills were led by Shane O'Neill, and the MacDonnells were led by the three brothers, James, Sorley Boy and Angus. James and Sorley were taken prisoner, and Angus was killed. James died of his wounds in a dungeon, but Sorley Boy was later released.

The MacDonnells were revenged at Cushendun two years later when they murdered Shane O'Neill.

There is a monument to another MacDonnell killed in Glentaisie – one John Roe MacDonnell. He appears to have gone as far as Glenshesk, to the Hollow of the Horses.

There was once a King of Norway named Nabghodon, and he lamented deeply the death of his wife. Courtiers told him that the women of Ireland were very beautiful, and that he should take one for his wife. Thirty men proceeded to Rathlin, where they saw a great palace, and they decided to stop there. It was not long before they saw a lady – the most handsome of the children of Adam – who had clear blue eyes, curling hair and a pleasant voice. She and her band of female attendants sat in an enchanting glade. This was Taisie Taobhkheal ('the princess of the white side'), daughter of Donn, King of Rathlin and descendant of Dagdha, King of the Tuatha Dé Danann. The strangers wanted the princess as a bride for their king, but they were refused. She had already been promised to one Congal. Relations were strained, but the strangers were provided with hospitality, and the next day they set sail for home.

Congal, who was wanted to lead Ireland, was at this time warring with Fergus McLeide.

When the King of Rathlin heard of an army being prepared by the King of Norway to take Taisie by force, he at once got in contact with Congal. Congal, accompanied by many chiefs, went immediately to Rathlin to marry Taisie, and to help defend the island. The Norwegians came as the celebrations were taking place, and a fight took place. Nabghodon was killed by Congal, and this led to a complete rout of the invaders.

Congal now went out to ask for a piece of land from Fergus

McLeide as a present for his wife, and as a symbol of peace between Fergus and himself. Fergus consented, and Taisie was given the area now known as Glentaisie. Here her father built her a palace called Dun Taisie. Today it is thought that the palace built for her was the great fort of Broomore under the shadow of Knocklayd.

Rathlin Island has seen many battles in its long history, but today many people live there peacefully. The island is divided into two, and the people are referred to by two different names: there are the Lower-end *'Cuddins'* and the Upper-end *'Forrins'*. *Cuddins* were fish fry and *forrins* were seabirds. Today the main language spoken is English.

Sydney Bell wrote a poem called 'By Rathlin Sound'. He wrote that his soul would come winging across the many miles between high cliffs that he loved, and here at last, like the great fulmar settling on her nest, he would find peace. Dear God, let it be. He would be free from the body's drag, to skim the waves, and to glide on snowy pinions down the wind or cling to pinnacles in the sun – this would be his heaven.

In the Tripartite Life of St Patrick it is recorded that he journeyed to the Glens, and his nose bled on the way. His flag, the Lec Patrick, was raised there, and the place is named Strath Patrick to this day. Domnach Patrick was its former name. Patrick stayed there on a Sunday; this was his only church in the region.

There is a theory amongst Patrican scholars that the Glens referred to were the Glens of Antrim, and the tribe referred to was the Muinteamhar, eighth in descent from the Cairbre Riada, who ruled in the Murlough area.

Near Torr Head is Leckpatrick. O'Laverty believed it had a special status, and he wondered if this was the church founded by the saint. The townland of Strath, or Straid, is nearby. In a field near the church is a Goolan stone, which is supposed to have the impressions of Patrick's knees. Inispollan also borders Culfreightrin, founded by the saint. There is a theory that the wood of Foclut may be in this area, for there is a townland with a similar name – Faughil. The Catholic church at Inispollan is the only Catholic church in the diocese to occupy an ancient site.

We come now to the story of Kieran. It seems that the community of Layd was badly affected by the Great Famine of the mid-nineteenth century. St Kieran approached the Abbot of Ardclinis, explaining that it would be another month until their corn would be ripe, and he asked for their prayers. The Abbot told Kieran to look across the bay, and he pointed out that his corn was already ripe. Kieran saw the yellow patches of ripened grain, and he went home praising God. He and his monks reaped the crop, and the place to this day reminds us of the miracle. Moneyvart means 'the moorland of the reaping'. It is thought that this Kieran is the same as Kieran of Clonmacnoise since their feast days are the same – 9 September.

St McKenna is another famous saint of the Glens. He is associated with the founding of the ancient church of Ardclinis mentioned earlier. The name of this saint might be Mo Enna, and this seems to link him with St MacNissi, whose other name was Enan. On the ditch opposite the church are many white stones called cahir McKenna (McKenna's cahir).

During the ninth century the Vikings became powerful in parts of Ulster, but they suffered a great deal when their leader, Turgesius, was overcome by Niall, King of Ulster. The last survivors of the Danes were said to have been an old man and his son, who fled before the invaders. They took refuge at Garron Point on the Antrim coast. The two had a special secret – how to make beer from heather. When, at length, they were captured, they were told that their lives would be spared if they revealed their secret. The father said that he would only reveal it if first his son was slain. This transpired. Then the old man, too, asked to be slain, saying that he would take his secret with him to the grave; and so the recipe was lost for ever.

Nearly every Irishman has heard of Finn MacCool, but his exploits are also told in Scotland and the Isle of Man. In Western Scotland several places are named after him, including Fingal's Stair in Argyllshire, and Fingal's Seat at the head of Portree Loch. Finn's father is said to have been the leader of the Fianna and to have been killed by a rival who was head of Clan Morna. They lived in the wild woods in a tree house, and Finn grew up large and strong, skilled in running, swimming and leaping – a true giant.

He acquired wisdom from eating the Salmon of Knowledge, caught for him by an old man fishing in the River Boyne. Later, an Ulster smith made a wonderful sword, which Finn earned after working for the smith for over a year. The name Finn was given to him by his enemies, who remarked, "Who is the fair one?" From that day Finn was his name. He later won the leadership of the Fianna and was praised for his bravery.

Many deeds are attributed to him – for example, the building of the Giant's Causeway and the throwing of a piece of land at a rival giant, giving rise to Lough Neagh and the Isle of Man.

In the parish of Loughguile there is a townland called Lavin, which is said to have called his name after Finn was dead. Before he was buried an old women took his hand and said, "The hand of Finn." The place was thereafter known as the Hand of Finn. There used to be a large stone called Finn MacCool's Stone, but it was removed some time ago. There were also three other stones at the spot. In 1813, it is recorded, one Andrew Duncan removed one of them and discovered a cinerary urn.

Finn loved his hounds, and the tale of Doofin in Glenshesk tells of his love for Bran. His other hound's name was Skolaun.

Oscar, Ossian's son and Finn's grandson, was killed in battle. He was greatly mourned by Finn. A little poem tells the tale of Oscar, slender and fair: may he run wild . . . and Oscar lies slain to rise no more. Finn only wept twice: at the death of Oscar and at the death of Bran.

There is a tradition that Flora MacDonald brought Bonnie Prince Charlie to spend a night with her kinsmen in the Glens after his flight from Scotland. Possibly he stayed at an old ruined house near Castlegreen, called Mullards. There may also have been a large house at the top of a mysterious avenue behind Mullards. He may have stayed there, but no trace of the large house remains. The place has been referred to as Castle Green. In the old graveyard of Templeastra, Port Bradden, there is a gravestone erected to the memory of a servant of Flora MacDonald who died while accompanying her on a journey to the Glens. Perhaps the old castle was razed because it had sheltered the prince. In one corner there is a mysterious avenue, and the water in the well was sweet. This area was owned by one Captain MacDonnell who had fought with James II. When he followed his King into exile, his lands were forfeited. Perhaps he owned the large house, and it was subsequently destroyed.

Another gravestone in the old churchyard states that it is the burying place of her husband. Perhaps it was not *the* Flora MacDonald, as the name on the stone is not the name of her husband. Flora MacDonald is said to have saved the life of Prince Charles Edward Stuart on 28 June 1746. She was arrested after the event and imprisoned until July 1747. Later she married another MacDonald and went to America, but she returned to Skye, where she died. She had seven children and left many descendants.

The Glens of Antrim Feis, held in the little town of Waterfoot (Glenariff) was spread over a few days. Days were set aside for the language competitions, singing and music, and the celebrations finished with sports and dancing on the first Sunday in July. The Glens of Antrim Feis began in 1904, sponsored mainly by Margaret Dobbs of Cushendall and Ada McNeill of Cushendun House. Dr Douglas Hyde was present at the first one, as was Roger Casement. The story goes that Roger Casement brought by boat all the inhabitants of Rathlin Island to Waterfoot for the first Feis. He presented each with half a crown to spend at the festivities. It was indeed a red-letter day for the people of Rathlin, for their own harper became the champion harper of the Glens that day.

It was hoped that the Feis would travel round the Glens, and at times it was held in such centres as Glenarm, Carnlough and Ballycastle, but Waterfoot was the most central place, so the Feis became established there. People travelled from all over Ireland to enjoy the fun and competitions, and certainly the event has been important in keeping the Irish language alive in the Glens.

Siobhan ni Luain has written a poem entitled 'The Feis of the Glen'. She wrote that when she was young she took a day off. The sun shone all day, and she went one morning to the Feis with everyone watching. She wore a linen frock with cuffs of lace. She wore a yellow hat and a cherry bow. The sun shone as it had never shone before over sea and glen and on the bright waterfall. She was sometimes wise, sometimes clever; she knew all things. Through the green, golden glen the birds were singing, and all the little birds were in tune with her. The pipers in their saffron kilts were swinging down the Glen's foot where it meets the sea. There were interesting prizes, for she knew everything she wanted to know, for she was sure of things at the beginning, for she wore that yellow hat with a cherry bow.

Chapter 10

Traditions

As can be seen from the account of the Hyndman family, there was a great respect for fairies and things connected with them. Sometimes they were known as *groga*. In Glenshesk they were supposed to be responsible for the building of the church. A dialect dictionary tells us that in Antrim and Down a *grogan* is a kind of fairy, two feet high and very strong. It helped farmers with harvesting and threshing but was offended if it was offered any recompense.

Smooring was the custom of burying live turf in the ashes of a fire last thing at night. This was done to appease the fairies, who would be angry if there was no fire for them to sit at through the night.

Harry Browne collected a lot of folklore in the Glens for the *Ulster Journal of Archaeology*. In a cottage not far from Glenarm a young man told him that although he himself had never seen the wee folk he would not like to conjecture that they did not exist. He remembered his grandfather, who had said that he had seen them more than once. Indeed the old man watched a fight between them. "Aye," he said, "you were talking about fairy thorns." He said that he and a man from Cushendall, not more than six months before, were having a drink together after the fair. The man told him that he had cut down a fairy bush, and the next day when he got up out of bed his face was round at the back of his neck. From that day on, whenever he went anywhere near where the old thorn bush had grown he fell about all over the place.

A woman in Glendun wanted to clear a field of fairy thorns in order to build a house. The lorries broke down, workmen got injured and the house was never built.

Another person told a story of his experience whilst he was living on a farm in Glendun: The man wanted to take down a *skeogh,* or fairy thorn, that was on the farm. He hagged away at it, but after a blow or two the blade 'turned'. He obtained another axe, and when he struck the tree blood came out. That finished him. He went home and went to bed. By the following morning all his hair had fallen out, and he had to wear a wig for the rest of his life.

Another man cut a *skeogh* and his hair turned white overnight. His son wanted to build a small house to keep rabbits in, so he chose a site and started to dig, not realizing that he was near a *skeogh*. Suddenly, he had a voice saying, "Don't dig here!" but he paid no attention, thinking he was hearing things. Again the voice said, "Do not dig!" This time he was sure that a friend was playing a trick on him, and he went to look for him. But no one was there. When he started again the voice became louder: "Don't dig here!" He stopped at once and headed home with his spade. He gave up the idea of building a hut on that spot.

A friend later mentioned to him that his mother and sister had heard fairy music as they were coming from a ceilidh at a neighbour's house late at night. It was, they said, the sweetest music in the world.

An old man remarked, with a twinkle in his eye, that the fairies had all gone away because the people were so bad.

Fairies must have lived close to the houses of people, for another story tells of a woman who was staying at the house of a friend. She had just washed the dishes, and as she was about to throw the dishwater out near the door she heard a wee voice call, "Don't throw it there; it will go down the chimney."

Professor Estyn Evans describes a fairy thorn as one not planted by man, but which grew on its own, typically on some ancient rath or cairn. Occasionally a group of fairy thorns or 'gentle trees' is found. It is generally held that a fairy thorn is one where the trunk is single for long way up, not branching or dividing near the ground. Fairy thorns are thicker and rarer than ordinary thorn trees.

Harry Browne wrote that there was once a fairy thorn growing in a hedge by the roadside. It had stood alone at one time, but the road had been driven through the field, and, to make a hedge, more bushes had been planted. The local people always respected the tree, and it was never pruned with the rest of the hedge. Eventually it became a nuisance, and it was ordered that it should be cut down; but the old roadman refused to have anything to do with such sacrilege. At length the old roadman died and a younger man took his place. He cut down the fairy thorn, and some of its branches were mixed with others and given to the neighbour to put under his haystacks. Two months later the neighbour's daughter died.

H. Browne wrote a little poem called 'The Sea-Song'. He had often heard the Glens folk call to the seals which used to gather on Connell Rock on a summer's day. As they swam round the rock they used to sing, and their songs echoed like the speech of men. Their strange siren songs drifted on the air, as they called, perhaps to someone in the Glens. Perhaps it was the soft Gaelic tongue that all the Glens folk used to know, or perhaps it was something older still. Whom were they calling? Who was it that knew the songs and answered not the soft and sad refrain? It would be someone they wanted, someone they loved and missed – one who had gone and come back again. Their cries haunted the summer days. She who was lost did not answer them, so the seals come to the Connell Rock no more.

Stories about the Hare Woman are common throughout Ireland, including the Glens. It is said that she could change herself from an old woman into a hare and suck cows' milk. Shooting at her was no good; the only solution was to load the gun with silver sixpences. Once a hare was shot in the leg, and on the same evening an old woman was carried into her house with a bullet in her leg.

One story tells of a horseman riding along a road in the moonlight. All of a sudden, he saw an old woman standing upon a hillock with her arms stretched out in front of her. She called to him to come to her. He did not know the old woman, but he pulled up his horse and, as he was of a humorous disposition, he thought that he might as well have some fun. He threw up his arms and told her to come to him. At that his knee boots were filled with milk. He put spurs to his horse and he did not stop until he was in his own house.

Dobbs tells of a man who saw fairies dancing under a thorn, and he knew he was in for bad luck. He suffered the following winter when his hut was hit by lightning. His family were in terror. The storm hit far and wide, but he thought that it was meant especially for him. It is interesting to note that there were Neolithic men called Fir Bolgs, who were said to have hidden in underground dwellings when conquerors arrived in Ireland. From this time the folk memory of curious wee men may have originated. Fairy means 'the men of the hillock'.

Foxgloves grow all over the Glens, and they are sometimes called fairy thimbles. Other names are fairy gloves or folks' gloves. The hawthorn is also called the hag-thorn, and its berries are said to be associated with sacrificial drops of blood. The ash leaf and the rowan berry are protective aids.

Whin grows in great quantities on the hillsides, and has been referred to as 'the curse of Ireland', but it does not seem to have fairy connections. During the famine their petals provided food for men and horses.

Complaints that have been cured by charms include erysipelas, warts, sprains and jaundice. The charmers did not ask for payment. Sometimes they used their powers to cure humans but could not cure animals, and vice versa.

Warts were caused to vanish by applying the juice of some herb. Another cure was to rub them with a potato that was then wrapped up and thrown away. Woe betide the finder of the parcel, for the warts would grow on him! Warts are curious, for they can appear or disappear overnight.

Jaundice was thought to have been cured by mixing the urine of the sufferer with soda or wheaten bread, which was then secretly fed to him. Sprains were helped by the tying-on of coloured thread.

There was also amongst the Glens folk a superstition that cows' milk could not produce butter for several days unless an old woman uttered a charm to 'take the blink away'. People were sometimes welcomed into the houses when she was charming, and she would 'take the blink off' their butter too.

Another story tells of cows being 'elf-shot'. It was said to be possible to see the place where the cow had been struck. At that point there would be a hole in the flesh, but the skin would be unbroken. Cows that have been elf-shot yield no milk until relieved by a charm. O'Laverty gave an interesting cure. He said that sick cattle were said to have been shot by fairies with the stone arrowheads which were frequently found in fields. The remedy was to make the cow drink a mixture of hot water and oatmeal out of a vessel containing a number of stone arrowheads.

If a person with the power to 'blink' admired a new litter of animals, it was always safest to give him one. When a cow gave birth to a calf, a little hay or straw was set alight around her to keep out the fairies. Another remedy for 'blinking' was to give the cow three mouthfuls of salt and water. What was left was emptied into a bucket on the hearth.

The 1835 Ordnance Survey states that there was a legend that a chapel would not stand in Ardclinis, for the walls had fallen twice in the building and the vessels which brought the slate and other materials were all lost. According to tradition, a hermit once cast a spell on the river at Ardclinis, and the belief is reinforced by the fact that there were very few trout in the river. It is also thought that a cock would not crow over the parish of Ardclinis.

There is some mention of the Glens of Antrim in *Ulster Folklore* by Jeanne Cooper Foster. People had at one time a fear that their soul might be captured if their photograph was taken. One woman did not want to be photographed, but she was later persuaded to hold a three-legged pot for it to be photographed.

A Ballycastle woman, when describing a banshee she had seen, said that it was a little wizened and red-haired woman who ran before her in a bog. She wailed and wrung her hands with anxiety.

Around Ballycastle a similar type of fairy is called a *groghach*. It is described as being large and uncouth, with a hairy skin. It would disappear when rewarded for its labour.

The folklorist Sam Henry has recorded a story connected with Ballyvoy. It was said that a person whose mother's maiden name was the same as her husband's was the proper party to point a gooseberry jag at a stye in the eye to bring about a cure. People on Rathlin Island have a variation of this. They say that a magical charm could only be worked by a woman whose parents were of the same name. It was also said that a rope of hair wound round a churn would bring back the butter to the milk of 'blinked' cows.

The holy well called Sunday Well, near Cushendall, was visited for the cure of diseases, chiefly by children. A little pebble would be thrown into the well and a pin stuck into a piece of cloth beside it. Thousands of these shreds may be seen there, but the practice is in part dying out, and the water is now used to turn a corn mill. According to tradition, all the places with the name Sunday Well were founded by St Patrick, and their foundations took place on Sundays.

There is a poem by W. Clarke Robinson about Glenarm and the Antrim coast. It begins: Fairy thorns in fields or fen are passed in silent fright. While walking in that yawning glen a glimmering light can be seen, where roofless ruined Majey's Mill stands mid the lowering flood. Nightly ghosts and witches chill the lonely traveller's blood. Youths on Easter morning would rise to meet the dancing sun. They would gaze until their eyes believed the dance had begun. Some at Easter or May Eve through the green meadows would roam. They might bring catkins home. They might dye their eggs with bloom of whin, and throw them high and watch. They would play 'round the rung', 'tig out' (or 'in') and kiss the girls they caught. They might burn nuts at Halloween, and duck for apples in water, or bite at crossing sticks. The poem goes on to say that none dared to eat blackberries when Halloween was past, for then the Devil had cast worms upon them. Christmas rhymers then would play St George or Robin Hood, and they would light the logs of wood.

The Christmas rhymers may have been known around Glenarm, but it is a custom not known in the Glens farther north.

St Brigid's crosses vary in shape, the most common being the three-legged type. They are woven out of rushes and are fashioned on St Brigid's Eve (the last day of January). The cross was originally a pagan symbol, but it has taken on a Christian significance. They were hung over the doorways of houses or in byres to protect the buildings from fire and to safeguard their occupants from evil spirits. Brigid was a cowherd, and she had a personal interest in cattle. In an old account written for a Naturalists' Field Club outing we learn that an old lady in a cottage in Glenaan had a St Brigid's cross made from rushes. She called it "the *cailleagh*". Such crosses were plaited left over right. In the Glens it was once the tradition to make a small bed of rushes and place it near the fire on St Brigid's Eve so that the saint could come in and rest.

Dobbs said that people were not as strict in keeping holy days as formerly. In general holy-day observance was troublesome. The day was spent in the pub and little was done the next day. When two or three holy days occurred in a week, it was a fine excuse for week's idleness.

The May Festival, or Gaelic Beltane, was a time of many magic beliefs and superstitions. If you placed a snail under a bowl on May Eve, the next morning you could read the mind of your future marriage partner. Mayflower used to be crushed to make juice with which a cow's udders were washed. In other places the juice of buttercups was used as a protection or to ensure a good milk supply. May dew was considered a great make-up for the ladies. Sprigs of rowan, which had protective qualities, were stuck in middens and over byres to protect farms from wicked fairies. May flowers were gathered on 1 May and placed upon doors and windows. A short poem reads that it was on Beltane Eve that copses and dells were ransacked for their flowers to deck the following day's feast. Each gate and door with garlands and green leaves was covered over.

The last sheaf of corn is called the *cailleagh* ('the old woman in the Glens'), but in other parts of Ireland it is called the 'churn' or 'hag'. Many games and ceremonies were connected with it: The sheaf was left standing uncut, then plaited in three strands. Now followed a competition to see who could cut it by throwing sickles at it. This game had some early connections with the worship of the Corn Spirit. The word *hare* is sometimes used instead of *cailleagh* and the harvest festival itself is sometimes called the Hare Feast. The idea of the Corn Spirit was so real to children in the Glens that they stood around waiting to see it run away to a farm where the corn was not yet cut. In Scotland a strip of corn was always left uncut on each farm so that no farmers would have the ill luck to be last to cut the corn. The *cailleagh* was then hung in the kitchen, and it was said to ensure that the animals wouldn't go hungry on that farm.

At Cushendall, fairs were held eight times a year. Girls going to the fair used to carry their white stockings and good shoes in their hands until they were nearly there. Then they washed in the nearest stream. Everyone dressed up for the big day. On the Coleraine road the girls washed at a well called the Sprout on their way to the Lammas fair, but today there is no trace of the well.

May rents were paid in August by the supplying of butter, and November rents were paid in February by the selling of pork.

The Lammas fair today is associated with Ballycastle. Long ago this feast was held on 1 August throughout Ireland, but now it is held on Lammas Sunday – the last Sunday in July. It is also known as Garland Sunday or Bilberry Sunday. This occasion marks the end of summer and the beginning of autumn. Offerings of flowers and fruit were made at holy wells and the folk gathered at some high place for games and fun. Blaeberries (bilberries) were gathered in the Glens.

The Old Lammas Fair is celebrated on the last Tuesday in August, extended recently to the Monday. (It could be that the late harvest in the region influenced the date.) The fair may have its origins in the need to bring supplies from Scotland to assist the MacDonnells when they were fighting in the Glens and the Route. The men of Islay were regular visitors to the fair, and there are records of them coming until the late nineteenth century.

A fair was held at Ballycastle to celebrate the coming of age of Gillespie Feacle, the MacDonnell heir. There were days of games and celebrations, but sadly a bull broke loose and wounded Gillespie. He later died off his wounds on Rathlin Island, but he had already married and his wife gave birth to a male heir to carry on the line. There used to be six annual fairs at Ballycastle, held near the ancient castle of Dunaneanie ('the fort of the fairs').

The Old Lammas Fair has an unbroken history of over 300 years. Today it is still a popular event, drawing many tourists to Ballycastle. There is a brisk trade in livestock (horses, sheep and cattle). Stalls are set out in the Diamond. Yellow man, a sort of hard yellow toffee, is one of the fair's specialities. The recipe is closely guarded. Little biscuits called hard nuts were also sold at the fair. Today, as well as the traditional fare, a great variety of modern goods is sold. The stalls all do a good trade and there is a festive atmosphere. In a nearby street, horses are trotted up and down to show their points, and many bargains are struck with the slap of a hand.

In country areas, where people did not travel very far, the Lammas fair was a great event. A hundred years ago it used to last a week, with dancing and all sort of amusements. Almost the entire population of Rathlin Island crossed over to Ballycastle regularly for the fair, bringing cattle to sell. If the weather was bad, they did not mind having an extra few days in the town.

We must pay tribute to another speciality of the fair – dulse. Large quantities of this edible seaweed were gathered locally for sale to the fair-goers. John McAuley, a bog-oak carver who preserved many old songs, is above all remembered for the famous song 'The Ould Lammas Fair'. It goes: The Ould Lammas Fair, were you ever there? Did you treat your Mary Ann to dulse and yellow man?

Halloween was a night when the living felt the dead quite close at hand. Strange things happened. If at midnight a girl looked over her shoulder into a mirror, she might see the face of her future husband. An apple was peeled at Halloween and the peel was thrown over the left shoulder. Another superstition was that if a girl found two teaspoons in her saucer and heard a cuckoo next day, she might be married within a year. The first day of November was known throughout Ireland as Samhain. The festivities were partly, of course, to celebrate the return of those who had been away all summer on the high pastureland with the cattle (*booleying*). Samhain is also known as All Saints' Day.

All Souls' Day is on 2 November. It is wrong to equate All Saints' Day with All Souls' Day as is often done.

A bonfire and dressing up for children is still part of the fun, and there is still a certain atmosphere about Halloween; but the old traditions are dying out. Turnip lanterns are still made, but what is the reason? Perhaps it is to scare someone away. They are like empty skulls.

John Hewitt wrote a poem called 'The Wake' on the occasion of Dan Hyndman's death: The latch was snicked where one was dead, and the open coffin on the bed showed us the man we had come to see. We gave our greetings to the gloom. We found a seat against the wall, and his wife was hustled into the room where women were gathered. The turf and wick did not give much light, and the crouching shapes seemed much the same with anxious ears and sight. The talk was about the stock and of the harvest and about the distances men might walk, and of the dangers of our pampered state. One would rise and say goodnight. The smoking turf would flicker bright with each gust of air. Suddenly the only sound would be crickets at the grate, and James would hand around tobacco on a dinner plate.

Banshees are eerie spirits of doom. They belong exclusively to Ireland. The wailing of the banshee is supposed to presage death. Long ago in ancient Ireland there was a people called the Sidhe, who were feared for their mystical powers. The women of this tribe were noted for their wailing, and they gave their name to what we call the banshees or women of the Sidhe.

When someone died, the body would not be touched for an hour. Meanwhile all mirrors and pictures would be turned to the wall, the clock would be stopped and later the clothes of the dead person would be burnt. In all parts it was the custom to 'wake the dead' or have a wake. Friends and neighbours of the deceased gathered at his home. Visitors would go first into the room where the body lay, then they would place a hand on the corpse's brow to symbolize friendship between the living and the dead. Nowadays people at a wake eat and drink in great quantities. A supply of clay pipes used to be provided so that everyone could smoke together. The custom was in many ways a useful distraction for the relatives of the deceased.

An interesting story has been told in Cushendall about a wee woman. When her dead body was placed in her coffin, a plain wooden box, she did not fit it at all. She was so small that they thought the body might roll around in it.

Corpses were always taken out feet first, and a roundabout way to the churchyard was taken. It was believed that the spirits of the dead hovered about and might return to the house. The shutters were closed and the blinds were pulled down. All this was intended to confuse the spirit and stop it from returning. Dobbs described the events: Whenever a person died in a townland no work was done until the body was buried. Before a dead body left the house all the pins, etc. were removed and loosed to prevent the spirit being detained in Purgatory. Priests were often buried with their boots on. This information is derived from the customs of the Glens.

Weddings were often accompanied by horseplay. A wedding took place in Glendun, and the newly-weds had gone to their home up the glen, but that night some boys played some tricks. They fired guns and locked the bridegroom in a shed. After this they removed all the gates.

There is perhaps a connection between firing guns and ancient rites to drive away evil spirits from a new home.

If a pregnant woman arrived at a house, it was considered unlucky if the host did not greet her and provide her with a share of the meal. Parents would not rock their children in a new cradle, but they would send any distance for an old one. If they had to leave the child alone for even a minute, they would place a pair of tongs across the cradle or basket to stop the fairies from carrying it away. If a child did not cry when it was being baptized, they considered it a very bad omen. This information has also come from customs in the Glens.

A child born with a caul was said to be very lucky: it would never be hung, drawn and quartered, drowned in the sea or burnt alive.

The Glens have a character that is unique, for they are alive with nature's wild beauty. They capture the heart, despite the changes that have come to the Glens. The journey home to Ballygally from Ballycastle takes about an hour, and we pass through the nine glens, bidding them a fond farewell. We drive down the Antrim coast, looking out across the deep mysterious waters of the North Channel – an unrivalled view enjoyed by ancient and modern man alike.

Select Bibliography

Cahal Dallat: *A Tour of the Causeway Coast* (Friar's Bush Press, 1990).

Cahal Dallat: *The Road to the Glens* (Friar's Bush Press, 1989).

Felix McKillop: *Glenarm* (the author, 1987).

Heart of the Glens (The Causeway Initiative, 2002).

Jonathan Bell: *People and the Land* (Friar's Bush Press, 1992).

Lesley Whiteside: *Saint Patrick in Stained Glass* (Gill & Macmillan, 1998).

Maureen Donnelly: *Saint Patrick and the Downpatrick Area* (the author).

Maureen Donnelly: *The Nine Glens* (the author, 1987).

The Reverend George Hill: *An Historical Account of the MacDonnells of Antrim* (Archer & Sons, 1873).

R. H. McIlrath: *Early Victorian Larne* (Braid Books, 1991).